BY MICKEY HESS

GARRETT COUNTY PRESS

Garrett County Press First Edition 2008

This book is a work of creative nonfiction. The events in this book occurred in real life, although not necessarily in the order or form in which they appear here. Indiana University Southwest is not a real institution, but an imaginary place created by combining aspects of several different universities where Mickey Hess taught in the twilight of the 20th century and the dawn of the 21st. As imaginary places go, IU Southwest is relatively unimaginative. Unicorns do not roam there.
Also, Mickey Hess asked the real people in the book if they wanted him to change their names. Some of them did.

For more information address:
GARRETT COUNTY PRESS
www.gcpress.com

Printed in Canada.
GARRETT COUNTY PRESS BOOKS ARE PRINTED ON RECYCLED, ACID FREE PAPER.

Library of Congress Cataloging-in-Publication Data
ISBN 1-891053-02-7 (alk. paper)
PN1992.77.L67W66 2006
791.45'72--dc22

The publisher thanks Dade Darby & Jamie Schweser
for their help in realizing this project.

Big Wheel at the CRACKER FACTORY

BY MICKEY HESS

Spring Semester

One

I started working as a Freezee Pops ice cream vendor during my first semester as a faculty member at Indiana University Southwest. I had spent all week working on arrangements to bring two Icelandic writers to campus: reserving plane tickets and hotel rooms, securing funding from departments and offices all over the school. I saw the Freezee Pops ad right after I met with the Vice Chancellor, and I called their number still in professional mode, asking for more details about the job.

"Man, if you don't know what driving an ice cream truck is, it's just cruisin' around, sellin' cones."

As simple as they made it sound, I would have to sit through two training videos before they handed over the keys to the ice cream van. One was all about safety concerns, and the other they called "Sales Techniques." A guy who supposedly founded the company sat down on his desk and told the camera, "Kids want to spend their money. If you see a child has more money, try to nudge him toward a more expensive item. Remember, kids *want* to spend their money. I can't stress that enough. If a child goes home with an extra dollar today, then that will be one less dollar his mother gives him the next time your truck comes by." He looked smugly into the camera, folded his hands in front of his knee, and nodded twice. It was an awkward pause. I wasn't sure if he was trying to let that last message sink in, or trying to think of what he wanted to talk about next.

Freezee Pops Ice Cream is located in the shittiest part of town, surrounded by strip clubs and adult bookstores. The only connection I can make is novelties. The other businesses on South 7th Street sell vibrators and anal beads and we sell Oreo Chip Burgers and Bubblegum Sno-cones. They have broken neon signs that look as bright in the daytime as they are probably ever going to look at night. So many bulbs are blown that I can't really make out the names of the places, but I think one is called IRLS IRLS GIR. That one might be the Swedish strip club.

Freezee Pops doesn't really have a sign at all besides "No Trespassing." Steven, the owner, explained to me that drivers for other ice cream companies would sometimes climb the fences to sabotage his trucks. "I know it sounds ridiculous," he said, and it did. The Freezee Pops headquarters reminds me of a fortified compound, the kind of place where cult members would live. It's very secure, and very self-sufficient. They have their own garage and mechanic on site, and an enormous freezer with enough ice cream to outlast a standoff with the federal government. Steven only opens the gates twice a day: in the morning to let the drivers get into their trucks, and at night so they can return them. When he shows up late, all the trucks line up outside the strip club across the highway.

Steven put on his glasses when I handed him my application, but he seemed to peer over the top of them as he read. "Let's see ... three years teaching at the University of Louisville, one semester at IU Southwest ... you know how to drive a stick-shift?"

❖ ❖ ❖

Side jobs have been a necessity. Over the past three years I have taught every class I've been offered at pretty much every college or university in the Louisville, Kentucky area, but in the summer there aren't many opportunities. It's like trying to pick fruit in the off-season. Teaching in the summer hinges on how many students sign up for the class, so I don't know if I have a job or not until the morning the summer classes begin. I teach as adjunct faculty, as a part-time instructor, so even if my own class fills up, it can be taken over by a full-time professor if theirs doesn't. It's horrible. Fifteen minutes before I'm scheduled to teach, I can go from copying my syllabus to looking through the employment section of the student newspaper.

Teaching part-time you can have all the appearances of job respect. Outside work, people are impressed when you tell them what you do for a living. But on campus, you share a five-desk office with forty other people and get paid a flat, per class rate. No benefits, no health insurance, and around one-fifth of the salary a real professor would earn. It's the only professional position I can think of that works that way. You don't see any part-time hematologists or adjunct surgeons. You can't leave your doctor's office and see him two hours later making sandwiches at the place down the street. For the past three years, I've had to scramble for jobs, piece together all the classes I could find, and when there weren't any I worked as a waiter or a library assistant. I might teach until ten one night and be up at eight the next morning for my class at a completely different school. Sometimes I'd teach at three different universities in the same day. Any routine I settled into would be broken within fifteen weeks, when the semester ended. Part-time jobs in the summer were an extension of that. I ended my classes in April and two weeks later I was waiting tables at Acapulco Bar and Grill.

During the fall and spring I taught courses in college writing, but in the summer I learned how to pour tea from the side of the pitcher and convince people to try our Mexican Eggrolls. At the end of the night, I'd take all the cloth dinner napkins off the tables and replace them with blue paper napkins for lunch. Then I'd bring out the clean silverware and marry the condiments, which means pour all the near-empty bottles of ketchup or mustard into fuller bottles to make it look like we'd just bought them, and wipe them down so they didn't look as old and crusty as they really were. The restaurant had these little plastic connectors that went between bottles to make sure nothing was spilled. "Ketchup to ketchup or mustard to mustard," the manager told me. He had this joke he always made about mixed marriages. Acapulco was one of those upscale Tex-Mex bar and grill kinds of places. It wasn't a chain, but it was too fancy to offer you free chips and salsa. I could watch people as I handed them the menu and they realized it was pricier than they'd expected. They'd nod in sort of a slow acceptance, and then watch things very closely to make sure they got what they were paying for, or maybe hoping to catch a slip-up that would keep them from having to tip, or to pay for their meal in the first place. People might send back a margarita because of too much or not enough salt. "I wanted salt on the glass, not *in* the margarita," but the free meal situation didn't come up too often. The owner was pretty discouraging. The only time she actually told me to make the offer was when somebody found a thumbtack in her salad.

On breaks I worked on lesson plans, put together my syllabus for the fall semester. The other servers used to make jokes, warn me that some night my students were going to come into the restaurant and I'd have to card them and refill their Diet Pepsis. It wouldn't have happened, though. I never carded anybody. It just never occurred to me until it was too late, like when those prep school kids gave me the thumbs-up when I brought them a margarita. I got to know the rest of the servers and dishwashers pretty well. Most of them were college students, half of them studying to be teachers themselves, so we had no problem identifying with each other. The cooks, though, seemed a little mistrusting of me, like they weren't sure what I was doing there. They were nice enough, really. They just always made me feel like the new guy. I don't know, maybe they should have been a little suspicious of people. They were always buying pot out the back door of the kitchen from some kid who came by on a bicycle.

My job at Acapulco paid my rent through the summer, and sometimes actually exceeded what I got paid for teaching. So it was back and forth, restaurant kitchen to the English Department.

❋ ❋ ❋

I grew up in times that taught me that it never pays to care about something, and that effort outside your personal artistic endeavors leads only to exploitation. Passion for starting a band, writing a zine, running your own record label — all this was ok — but caring about a job was in no way acceptable. Jobs were best tolerated, sat through with as little responsibility as possible. And a career? Just a job with more headaches.

I've been teaching at universities since I was 23, but teaching part-time has never felt like a true occupation. My friend Chad even pointed it out, how weird it was for one of us to have such a serious job as teaching college. But it was part-time, and it didn't have all the negative, soul-crushing aspects that usually come along with someone's first serious job. Beyond teaching, my only other obligation was office hours, which seemed unfair since I didn't have an office (seriously, at one school I didn't even have a mailbox, just the bottom half of a cardboard box with MICKEY written in magic marker). I did most of my work at home, all the lesson plans and research and responding to student papers. Chad, who knew even in seventh grade that he was going to medical school, used to make fun of me. He understood about jobs and success before I even started to think about it. Chad has known me longer than almost anyone has, and he pointed out how funny it is that I'm becoming such a professional, how strange to see me actually care so much about teaching, actually put so much time into it after I'd laughed at him for owning a planner. "I'm really impressed," he said, and I couldn't tell if he was being serious or sarcastic. The last time he'd said he was impressed with something was when I showed him this cool breakdancing move it took me a whole year to figure out.

But there was some responsibility to it. I could feel it creeping in. Teaching felt different than working at Acapulco. I cared about what kind of job I did. I felt like I could be good at it, and with four schools within driving distance, I could piece together a decent living. One semester I bet another instructor to see who could teach the most classes at once, and at how many different places. I capped out at seven, across four different schools, but he did ten. *Ten.* It was insane.

Teaching so many classes, though, started to feel like a job. Between teaching and commuting, I don't necessarily have a lot of time left to be anything besides a college instructor. It's becoming a part of me, a big piece of who I am.

So how do I deal with this new responsibility? By driving an ice cream truck.

❖ ❖ ❖

When I woke up this morning at 8:30 AM, all I wanted to do was stay in bed with Danielle and it took every ounce of determination to keep me from calling Freezee Pops and saying forget this whole ice cream idea. But Danielle talked me into it. She's good about that. Anytime I think, "This is crazy, should I be doing this?" she's right there to assure me I should. She knew that if I didn't go I'd be depressed for the rest of the day. I could live without the money — it's something else I need from this ice cream job. This semester has moved too quickly. It's almost March, almost spring break, and I look back and all I can see is classrooms, student papers, my fucking computer screen. And that isn't what's scary.

What's scary is that when I look forward, I see the same thing.

So I got up, brushed my teeth, and drove out to South 7th Street. Steven handed me a Driver Certification Quiz. "You need to see the videos again?"

The training videos are basically propaganda, although "Safety First" does feature a man in a clown suit who illustrates how drivers should check behind their trucks before backing up. He acts this out in exaggerated mime-like motions while a voice-over explains every step the clown is taking to make sure everyone remains safe and happy. After this brief safety message, the company's founder steps back into the picture to share some of his personal insights on the ice cream business — how to get in good with local business owners so you can hit their parking lots on employee breaks, and how to collect empty wrappers from kids so apartment lawn crews don't complain. But what really sticks with me is the advice the founder leaves us with: "Now I do want to see my drivers motivated, but motivating you is something I can't do. You have to be self-motivated to succeed. Remember, the happy, smiling people in life are the successful people."

The advice from some of the veteran drivers is more direct. "Start out in your black areas," one of them tells me. "That's where you make your money, in the projects. But you don't want to be caught out there after dark." This guy is huge. He looks like he might subsist entirely on his frozen inventory. Like most of the drivers who have been here for a few years, he's starting to develop a humpback from too many hours ducked under the low ceiling of the van. He walks over to the giant map of the city that takes up an entire wall of the office. While Steven outlines my route, they both point to specific spots I'll want to watch out for. "This one's rough," they say. "We had a guy get robbed out at this one twice. It's a crack neighborhood." I nod and try to act interested, without revealing that most of these are places Danielle and I have lived at one point or another.

✳✳✳

Driving an ice cream truck in February may not be the best idea. I spend most of the weekend making slow unproductive circles. My ice cream route is kind of like a tour of our old neighborhoods, except stopping to sell ice cream here and there. Safety Rule #6 is "No passengers at any time," but I stop and pick up Danielle before I go anywhere. It wouldn't be any fun without her. What's the excitement in being the ice cream man if there's no one to enjoy it with you? She's still in bed when I pull up, bells clanging. It's 11 AM, and we have the entire day ahead of us. Truthfully I don't think I could do it without her help. We work out a system where I'm responsible for the front of the truck, driving and handling interactions with customers, while she rings the bell and searches through the big freezer for Maple Nut Crunches or a Space Face Cookie. Her job is definitely harder. All day Danielle stands at a 75-degree angle, knocking her head into freezer doors trying to dig out the Astropops.

Danielle and I have been married for six years, or seventy-eight months. We got married for fifty dollars, in the living room of our HUD apartment, two months after my twentieth birthday. We celebrate our anniversary every month on the 23rd, and we celebrate birthday weeks — seven days of birthday fun — in late June and July. We celebrate a second, yet in no way subordinate, Halloween in June. At night Danielle sleeps on her side, pinned between my outstretched limbs (think Da Vinci) and our two cats, who insist on sleeping across the bed instead of longways, like people. With two pets already, Danielle asked if I wanted to adopt a three-foot iguana. I did. The iguana has its own room.

We purposefully leave the housing projects for the end of the day and waste an hour cruising through the park, temptingly keeping pace beside runners. Finally we park and eat Chocolate Eclairs at the top of this huge hill until even the health-conscious can resist no longer. Just the fact that we're in an ice cream truck adds this air of humor to everything we do. Getting change at the laundromat, listening to Dre and Snoop on the radio, turning it up as loud as the truck's speakers can handle. I'm the ice cream man.

Everything I do today feels different because I'm the ice cream man. The ice cream man pumping gas into his van. The ice cream man using the gas station restroom. We drive past a sidewalk sale at our favorite record store just to show off the truck, but nobody waves us down. They just stare, wearing their scarves and jackets.

I think Freezee Pops was so free with the trucks today because it's a rainy February weekend. Steven told me that normally your first day you tag along with another driver, but he said he trusted me, that if I thought I could handle my own truck, it was mine for the day. The only good thing about driving in February is that Danielle and I are making the first round of the season. Kids haven't seen an ice cream man for so long that we're like the second coming. I can see them tense up like rabbits sensing danger. The bells take a split second to register, and then kids drop whatever they're doing, leave bikes in the middle of the street and run down the sidewalks screaming *"Ice cream may-nnn!"*

The hardest part of the job is keeping a constant lookout for kids. They jump in front of the truck out of nowhere, yelling for me to *WAIT!* while they run inside to get money. The Sales Techniques video taught me the strategy: first you drive through a neighborhood making no stops at all. Kids hear the bells and become frantic like there's no way they're going to find money in time. So while they're scrambling around begging parents for change and trying to alert all their friends to your presence, you're making a slow loop back around to where you started, and this time through you drive really really slowly.

Another thing the video taught me is that it's important to recognize your repeat customers. One kid we sell to still has ice cream on his face from the day before. He rides up on a scooter and offers me two wadded dollars and a handful of sticky coins. This kid never names off the ice cream he wants. He just points to the pictures on the side of the van and sticks his hand back in his mouth. He pockets his two Cherry-

Banana Pops, but tears into his Pokémon Stick right away. He unwraps it and clenches it in his two fists like it's the Holy Grail. Before he takes a bite, I hear him say to himself "This is so *cool*!"

After I drop off Danielle at home and return the truck, I learn how to check the inventory in my freezer and separate my cash into neat little stacks by denomination. I get to keep thirty-five percent of what I sold, minus seven percent for taxes, minus a five-dollar truck rental fee. Steven is encouraging. "A hundred and sixteen dollars — you didn't do bad for your first day!" Tomorrow, though, he assures me I'll sell three times as much.

Sunday morning I load my truck full of ice cream with Steven still cheering me on then I drive home to my apartment and go back to bed. When Danielle and I wake up, the sun is overhead. It has turned into a really nice day for February, 75 degrees and sunny and everyone's outside — Louisville's first glimpse of spring. But do I bag the huge sales other drivers had promised for my second day? Do I move Malt Crunch Bombs and Big Dippers and make a name for myself in Freezee Pops retail? No. I leave the truck in Cherokee Park for a few hours and go for a walk with Danielle. We blow yesterday's money on black bean burgers and molten chocolate cake. We only sell ice cream when it's convenient, when people approach *us*. This new sales strategy brings in around forty-five dollars, and I come home to read student papers all afternoon.

I had all these ideas for the truck, like getting a haircut before I returned it, putting my cat carrier and some laundry in the front seat like I'd been running errands all day. Or trading ice cream to some neighborhood kid to hide in the truck and play dead while Steven checks inventory, or starting a turf war with the Good Humor crew across town. In the end, though, I didn't follow through. My one great prank was at Jake's expense.

Jake and Carrie were married young like us, came from small towns in southern Kentucky like us. Danielle and I have known Jake and Carrie almost as long as we've known each other, so long that I catch us telling each other stories that I know we've told before, and we all react like it's fresh material. I can't tell sometimes if we're humoring each other or if we've actually forgotten. Our stories combine and merge in different ways in our minds. We remember things but can't agree on what order they happened in, or which ones of us were there at the time.

We drive past their apartment building very slowly, ringing our bells, and then we drive around the corner and park on a side street. We run up the stairs to Jake's apartment screaming *Come on, let's go! The ice cream man's outside!*

Even with all the energy we put into it, we still can't budge Carrie, who is genuinely suspicious of anything I do. But Jake scrambles to find some money and we rush him out the door and around back to where the truck is sitting vacant. Jake's getting anxious already. "Aw, there's nobody in it."

"We should break in." Danielle starts to pull on the door handle.

"Yeah, fuck it. I'm going to get some ice cream anyway."

The door pops open and we both feign surprise. "He left the keys in here!" I start the engine, but Jake's already gone. He's all the way around the corner, halfway back to his apartment. I watched him take one really long step backward with this sincerely conflicted expression on his face, like he was piecing together the situation, and then he decided to run.

In his mind, it was the last time he'd ever see me. He thought I was really doing it, hitting the road in a stolen ice cream truck.

❊ ❊ ❊

My few sales on Sunday are courtesy of my friends. I ring ice cream bells outside Chad's apartment and interrupt his weekly Dungeons & Dragons game. Chad has played Dungeons & Dragons since I met him in junior high. He was actually a nationally-ranked Dungeon Master (No. 12) two or three years ago, the same year of medical school he had to repeat. Chad's bookshelves place *Spells for Wizards* between toxicology textbooks and *Pharmacology Today*. Hearing ice cream bells, all his friends from med school and the comic book shop put down their dice and come outside to investigate.

By the time I return the truck that night, I'm ready to get out of the ice cream business. I line up my truck next to the others, lock the front doors and go out the back to plug in the freezer before I close the sliding back door. Something feels wrong. I have my inventory checklist — I remember turning on the interior light to check everything off and count my tiny bag of coins. It isn't until I am inside the main office that I realize what I've done. I have left the light on and locked the keys in the van.

I never look back.

Since I met Chad's friends in that context, it was only natural for them to assume ice cream man was my main gig. I see one of them a few weeks later and he asks, "How's the ice cream business?" I tell him about the demise of the job, and he's sincerely disheartened by it. "Oh man. What are you going to do now?"

"I don't know," I tell him. "Teach college?"

11

Two

Looking through student course evaluations from last semester, I get some ideas for how to enhance my skills in the classroom. In response to one of the survey questions — "Please comment on the instructor's style, enthusiasm, etc. Do you have suggestions for improvement?" — students offer the following:

Show your legs more.

He was always a happy guy, but sometimes he could be a prick.

I will take these into consideration.

I am teaching at four universities in a 30-mile radius: The University of Louisville, Spalding University, Indiana University Southwest, and Jefferson Community College. The time I'm not teaching, reading papers, or going to meetings I spend driving back and forth between downtown Louisville and Southern Indiana. The ice cream truck was a welcome distraction, even if it did entail even more driving.

And now that I'm out of the ice cream business, I am faced with some decisions. When you work as a part-time lecturer, at some point you have to stop and consider which approach you want to take to the job: will you be a permanent part-timer, accumulating as many employers as possible and working extra jobs on the side, or will you apply to PhD programs and hope for a tenure-track job and all the health insurance and job security that come with it? People do it both ways. There's a steady rotation of people in their twenties and thirties who teach part-time until they find something more stable or more lucrative. There are bookstore managers and newspaper copy-editors making some extra cash on the side. Then, there are part-timers in their sixties and seventies, some of them retired from other jobs, some of them spouses of tenured professors, but some of them wrapping up three or four decades of part-time teaching, still paying for their own health insurance.

The question I have to ask myself is if I love teaching college enough that I'm willing to sign up for five more years of school and an increasingly slim chance at a tenure-track job? It's something I've given a lot of thought. I've talked to other part-time lecturers, who say do it now, get the PhD before I get old and burned out. I've talked to the English professors and researched the top programs, weighed the five courses I'm currently teaching against going back to school. I'm making more money now than I would as a grad student, but much less than I'd make as a real professor. But on the other hand, it feels like I'm turning my back on my idea of not letting a job define me, and on my plan to cancel out the responsibility of teaching college with stints driving ice cream trucks or stocking vending machines. It's not an easy decision. And just as I start filling out applications, IU Southwest offers me a job as a Full-time Lecturer.

❊ ❊ ❊

Full-time Lecturer is a new job title created strictly to keep the accreditation boards off a school's back. The way it works is that the accreditation agency expects a certain ratio of courses to be taught by full-time faculty. So to avoid losing their accreditation and still avoid paying for actual tenure-track professors, universities create a few of these low-level, low-paying positions that aren't technically part-time, but come with none of the benefits of being a professor. You can't get promotions. You can't get tenure. You teach the lower-level classes the professors won't touch, but at least you teach them all at one school.

Becoming a Full-time Lecturer is like becoming Head Dishwasher. You get the title, but with it comes more responsibility. It's one job at one school. It pays more, and I'll get some half-ass health insurance, but I'm not sure it's worth it. I'll be in limbo — required to go to faculty meetings upstairs but sent back to the basement to type the minutes on our community computer. There is talk of a new office, my own office, but for now I continue to share a desk.

The transitory nature of the job was what drew me to it in the first place, but I understand that I can't keep driving from campus to campus forever. The full-time position would end all that. At the same time, though, there's something I like about those words "temporary" and "part-time."

I haven't given them my answer.

IU Southwest is a commuter campus, a regional branch of Indiana University. There are no dorms or fraternity houses, but there are fraternities. They share a small Greek Life office that looks like it was not built for parties. A lot of the students are the typical 18-21 years old, but there is a strong contingent of nontraditional students, people who've been out in the world and already have jobs that pay more than mine.

The IU Southwest lecturers' office is dank and crowded. Forty of us in the basement, so close to the inner mechanisms of the humanities building that our room's temperature can't be regulated and we make do with thrift store fans and hand-me-down sweaters donated by retiring professors. The phone rings incessantly until it is taken over by Gordon, who's been here seventeen years and runs a side business selling curtains from the main office phone. Gordon's desk looks like he's stockpiling food in case we get trapped down here. Cases of ramen noodles and Save-A-Lot instant potatoes — he eats them hunched over his desk between classes.

Gordon is one of the few lecturers who seem to know that I work here, which somehow feels like an accomplishment. I can only guess that I've pulled it off by dressing in thrift store t-shirts and still being young enough to look like a student. One day I had been sitting at my desk for two hours and one of the other lecturers walked past and said, "Are you still waiting for your professor?"

Room 002 is hard to locate. Students walk right past the entrance because this couldn't *really* be their professor's office. Could it? Students who do find their way to our desks squeeze past stacks of English 101 portfolios from six years ago, from instructors long gone. Ghosts. The old-school lecturers entertain each other by reciting humorous grammar mistakes from student papers. It's awful, really, but they're burned out, tapped. They've read too many papers.

The permanence of a new full-time job makes me wonder if this will be me someday. Will I stop getting excited to read student evaluations? The prospect is more than depressing. When I was part-time, I didn't worry about this kind of thing. I was too busy driving from campus to campus, crossing my fingers for a summer class to keep me away from the restaurant. But at the same time, I liked the variety. The ice cream truck was a last-ditch effort at holding onto that kind of life. And now here I am, sitting at the same desk I was yesterday, waiting to go teach in the same classroom. If it feels like this much sameness already, how will it feel when I'm Gordon's age? If a career means accepting a permanent role, does it also mean that you accept that you will eventually become bored with that role, and thus bored with your life? Does it mean no more ice cream trucks? I try not to think about it.

❖ ❖ ❖

I was offered the full-time job at IU Southwest because I published an article about teaching. Doing research and publishing articles is the one thing professors are required to do that lecturers aren't, so it made me look like the perfect candidate, someone who'd do the whole job for half the pay. The article was about using surrealist games to teach research writing. The idea behind it was that most of what you do in college is write about other people — their books, their art, their ideas. But what if students could become the artists and writers and thinkers and then write about that? We did automatic writing and automatic drawing. We cut words out of the student newspaper and arranged them into random new sentences. And we wrote about all of it. During finals week we were going to play a baseball game using baby doll heads instead of baseballs, but the heads were expensive, and we were pretty much rained out. So instead we ate regular, non-surrealist pizza and played darts until the bar closed down and we said our goodbyes. I say it was eyestrain from reading seventy-five final papers, but some could have sworn they saw a tear.

I had the course description and some sample syllabi from past semesters, but I wanted to do something new, something that wouldn't look like every other English class these students had ever taken. I started writing the article because I was just waiting for someone in administration to come in and tell me not to teach it that way again. So in case they did, I had a theoretical framework, a defense, a manifesto. But the more I wrote about the class and the more I talked to those students, the more I understood that it really worked. I sent the article to a journal, they sent it to their reviewers, and they accepted it.

And here's where I got uncomfortable. I had been sending out stories to literary magazines for years, and I never got one acceptance. I wrote a novel and sent it to agents and small publishers, and I got "thanks, but not quite right for us." I published it myself and gave it away for free and a reviewer said it was "not a novel."

After all that rejection, I publish an article in a peer-reviewed academic journal on my first try. It wasn't that I wasn't excited about publishing the article. I was. I worked hard on it. But this was not how I had pictured getting my name into print. It's difficult to imagine two kids walking out of a public library somewhere, saying "Man, did you see that new issue of *Composition Studies*?" It was depressing to be better at something I just started than something I've worked so hard at for so many years, but still, I was excited about the contract to publish my teaching article. So excited that I started to believe it would fall through.

I have always sincerely believed that getting too excited about something can destroy it before it happens, that you can't celebrate until the actual moment of proof.

This keeps me from enjoying anything.

When I found out *Composition Studies* wanted to publish the article on my surrealism course, I looked over my shoulder to see if anyone else could have read the e-mail, the same way I do when I get less professional messages about "Dogfart Sluts!" or the "Shower-cam!!" I was taking my brief turn at the computer — *the* computer — in the part-time lecturers' office. Other teachers were lined up behind me, but I froze in my seat. I was afraid that if I moved, or breathed, my excitement could create a ripple in the universe, that it could jar a book off a shelf at DePaul University, crack the editor in the head rendering him useless to academics, and the presses would never start. So I kept quiet.

It would be months before the new issue came out, but I didn't tell anybody, not even Danielle. I had harassed her with my theories and reflections on teaching and made her read over drafts to see if they made any sense, but now I was suddenly, suspiciously quiet. When I reread the acceptance e-mail, I chewed my fingernails, muttered "Godfuckindammit" when I realized I'd sent in the wrong file on disk — "Surrealism Course Revised Version Seven" instead of Version Six. But Danielle was kept in the dark. By the time I told her, by the time the article finally came out, it had lost all impact on me. My moment to get excited was long past — I had suppressed it all until it disappeared. So I took pleasure in Danielle's surprise, experiencing what should have been my own excitement vicariously.

The problem with becoming a full-time college instructor is that I like teaching. I work hard at it, and I feel like I could be good at it. I was a student recently enough that I can still remember what didn't work. When I was a student, not much did. I spent most of my time ditching my classes to write stories. I believed that someday when people would ask me what I do, I'd reply "writer." "Full-time Lecturer" doesn't have quite the same ring. Now that I'm full time, teaching could rival writing, and I'm worried about that. All this time I'm spending teaching and writing about teaching was time I wanted to spend writing novels and memoirs. Writing was already crowding the time I had left for living. As good as I feel about being offered this new full-time job title, the idea of taking it also feels kind of like giving up.

❖❖❖

I used to feel different about this stuff. I didn't always feel so protective of my time. I was more interested in money than time. Growing up I saw my parents fight about money and borrow money and fight about borrowing money. I tried to act like I was in line by myself when Mom paid for groceries with food stamps. I wasn't the poorest kid at my school, but my friends all seemed to have more money than I did. I stopped eating lunch at school because I was embarrassed to show my Free Lunch Program card. And once, when our electricity got turned off due to unpaid bills, I had to carry a frozen pizza to our neighbor's house and ask if my sister and I could use their oven.

My mother was going back to school to finish her degree and teach elementary school. My dad ran his own auto body shop. He could have made more money working for a bigger auto repair place. Instead, he and his friends built his own garage behind our house. He hated working for someone else. He wanted to make his own hours and be his own boss, but I wanted to have more money. I wanted to have the things my friends had, so I resented him. I thought he was lazy. Mom wanted to be home to see her kids off to school and home when the bus dropped them off, but I told her I'd rather have a denim jacket with leather patches like the one my friend Chad wore.

I spent my weekends and summers working at my uncle's convenience store because I was bored and I wanted money. From the time I was twelve or thirteen I would help him stock shelves and break down boxes for recycling. He paid me in cash and I never spent any of the money. I kept it all in a shoebox and I'd count it from time to time, but I never spent it. Eventually my mom borrowed most of it to cover bills and never paid any of it back, but for a few months there I had a shoebox full of money.

So when I went to college I was going to major in business. I knew nothing about business other than that business makes money, which isn't so much the case with creative writing, the subject I was actually interested in. Either way, I didn't sign up for any business classes my first year. I chose classes on the basis of how much it surprised me that they actually fulfilled a credit. Fitness Walking. The History of Country Music. I became roommates with a guy named Shane who was six years older than me and loved nothing more than to point out things about me that struck him as stupid. My hair. My clothes. The music I listened to. My choice of major. When most eighteen-year-olds are moving into dorms with people their same age, I lived with a chain-smoking twenty-four year old paraplegic.

For Shane, living on his own was no new adventure. It was a habit. He'd been out in the world working in hotels and doing construction until he wrecked his motorcycle. He had a lot more courage than I did at eighteen. I don't think he would have ever gone to college if the Vocational Rehabilitation program hadn't paid for his books and tuition. He was only six years older than me, but it felt like he'd seen a lot in those six years. I felt like a little kid away from home for the first time.

Living with Shane was the first time I'd had to pay for rent and my own food, and my goal was to spend as little money as possible. I kept all my food receipts in a ceramic fish the old woman next door gave Shane to use as an ashtray. I even kept Taco Bell receipts in there. I had some idea that I would be able to deduct them from my taxes. When people came over to our apartment, Shane dumped my receipts on the floor to illustrate what a tightwad weirdo I was, and nobody disagreed. So I stopped saving receipts and tried to stop worrying so much about money. Shane was a huge influence on me, although the way things ended, it wouldn't have seemed that way. It's something I wish I had told him, but we don't really talk to each other anymore.

Then, the next year, two things happened. I moved out of Shane's apartment, and I met Danielle. Danielle and I met as roommates, each of us friends of a third, weird roommate, Chris, and having spoken to each other only twice before. The entire year, Danielle had a job for only 35 minutes. That was it. A few days after we signed the lease, she got a job at White Castle and Chris and I drove her to work. Half an hour later, she called us to come get her.

Chris worked part-time as a dishwasher that year, and I was living off student loans. I had developed this idea that the reason for going to college — at least one of them — was to work toward getting a better job than I'd be able to otherwise. So why work now for minimum wage and no benefits when I could live off government subsidy and pay it all back when I'm earning a higher salary? I always wanted to work it out mathematically to see if the wage difference covered the loan interest, but it seemed like it could take charts and formulas and everything. And I'm not very good at math.

So both of us wanted to live for free — that was one of the things that brought Danielle and me together, snickering after Chris headed out the door to wash dishes at seven AM when we hadn't even been to sleep yet. I had my loans, and Danielle's dad had bought her a car — combination graduation gift/guilt compensation — that she sold for rent money. Since all we wanted to do was be with each other, entertainment and sustenance came cheap. I wrote stories every night and never went to my classes. We would rather play darts or Scrabble or throw things off the balcony than leave the apartment. We did miss out on some concerts we couldn't afford, but we were never late with the rent.

We always knew it was temporary. At least I did. I understood that this period of student-loan limbo would be supported by some later stage in which I would trade my time, all this beautiful free time, for money. I was working toward something. And the limitations that fact placed on my student-loan years caused them to stagnate early. It was depressing the way I started to cling to them as I realized they were slipping away. I tried to sit very still to stop time from moving forward. Soon, Danielle enrolled in college herself, got her own loans, and went to class when I didn't talk her out of it. Chris locked himself in his room and stopped talking to us. We all moved out of the apartment eventually and we didn't see him for years.

❊ ❊ ❊

Danielle introduced me to quitting. She had quit high school, and she talked at least one of our friends into quitting college. He was homesick his first semester, and confused about what he wanted to major in. Danielle listened to him complain and said, "You should quit." These were things I would have never considered doing — I had been told I was going to go to college since I was in kindergarten. I was impressed with the way Danielle could turn away from something and never look back. But the longer I spent with her the more I understood how much her impulse to quit things was related to fear. When it came to trying something new, whether it was White Castle or going to college, she would convince herself that she couldn't do it, so she would quit. I didn't understand her anxiety. I couldn't believe someone so perfect could have so little confidence.

She introduced me to quitting and I introduced her to college. Danielle took her time in college, took semesters off here and there while I barreled through, taking as many hours as possible, even in the summer, because I believed there was something waiting for me when I left campus. There was not. That was who I was, always thinking I was working toward something, and I needed Danielle to make me see how much I was missing by thinking so much about the future. She needed me to show her what she was missing by not thinking about it at all. We balanced each other out, me encouraging her to attempt things and her telling me to quit them.

Three

Danielle thinks I should take the IU Southwest job. I don't know what to make of this. It was like I was waiting for her permission to turn down becoming a Full-time Lecturer, but that's not what she's giving me. "It sounds like you'd be doing the same thing you are now, but for more money. You like teaching. You'll still have time to write books in the summer." It makes sense. But it wasn't what I expected.

Let me explain something. Danielle and I are the same age, but she's just graduating this semester, the same semester as the first college students I taught. She took as few classes as possible and took time off when she got burned out, while I sped through in four years, making Ds in subjects like European Expansionism and Physical Geology because they didn't have enough to do with writing. I hadn't planned ahead to what I'd do after that. I guess I thought something would happen with my writing. Danielle's whole approach is taking things easy, but she understands that it doesn't work for me. I tend to overwork myself and then be disappointed with the results.

Danielle dreads graduating because it means having to look for a job. She believes there is no job out there that she will find satisfying. If I could write and get paid to write, I'd be completely happy, but I don't think she has anything like that. She said something about founding an animal sanctuary once, but it's not something she talks about very often or does any research on. To me, accepting a full-time job means accepting that teaching is what I do and I am no longer working toward anything. To her, it's just something you have to do.

I'm not doing her justice. My main weakness is describing people I know too well. It's easier to describe strangers. It's easier to describe Shane or Chris, old friends who are encapsulated in time, because I haven't seen them in years and in my mind they remain just like they were. But Danielle — I spend every day with Danielle, and there's so much to introduce, so much background and so many contradictions, and whenever I come to the truly important stuff I get tripped up in all these side stories which seem so much more urgent to tell:

Danielle was insightful enough to point out her meteorology professor when we went to a baseball game that got rained out before the first inning was over. "He must not know that much about meteorology," she said.

The top two items on Danielle's Christmas list this year were a monkey and a robot.

Danielle believes there's something lucky about 12:34, the only time on the clock when all four numbers line up in sequential order. We point it out to each other whenever we notice.

Danielle used to play solitaire for hours on the floor of our old apartment. She keeps showing me how to play, but I always forget.

Danielle does these cool black and white paintings on tiny, tiny canvases.

Danielle named our cat Semphonius, after an ancient Greek politician who was stoned to death while giving a speech.

Danielle got so high one time that she told me she couldn't walk home, and tried to get me to ask a cop for a ride.

She can watch the most violent horror films and laugh at the screaming and gore, but she cries when an animal dies on a nature show.

When Danielle draws pictures of animals, she always draws them smiling, and the smile looks exactly like hers.

Danielle believes that one peanut butter and jelly sandwich a day is the key to good health.

Danielle is much better at fixing cars than I am.

✳ ✳ ✳

I take my car to a mechanic named Ed Minton. "Minton Auto Repair," he says when he answers the phone. He runs the garage with his son, who never comes in before noon. When I first started taking my car there, Mr. Minton used to always tell me to drop it off at 8:30 or 9. Now it seems like he's given up, though — "Bring it in around 12:30." There seems to be a weird tension between them. The son always works on my car for some reason. Minton won't touch it himself. Every time I pick up the car, the speakers are turned all the way up and some heavy metal station is locked into my stereo.

My car is old but it's taken me to New Orleans and back, to countless hip-hop shows across the Midwest. It has made the commute to Indiana all semester, but shakily. Any day could be its last. I take it to Minton and son because they let me get by with the bare minimum, never hassle me to make all the repairs that would do anything beyond making the car run again. Some of this I can do myself — or more accurately, Danielle can do. She crawls under the car and I man the phone, relay instructions from my dad, 200 miles away.

Minton Jr. even seems surprised by it sometimes, like this morning —

"Did you know your cooling fan was rigged up with speaker wire?"

His dad makes a move like he's going to smack him in the back of the head.

"Well it sure as hell didn't come from the factory that way!"

After I drop off my car at Minton's shop, I'm still thinking about the job offer and if I'll still have enough time to write, if I could still go into a doctoral program and keep working toward something, if I could still keep my part-time jobs at other colleges.

To think, I need to walk. And if I'm walking, I might as well drop off more copies of my novel for people to pick up for free. So I head down Bardstown Road on foot, my backpack crammed full of the last remaining copies of the book I self-published. *El Cumpleanos de Paco* — random, interwoven true stories about living in shitty apartments. I paid just over one thousand dollars for the one thousand copies I printed, and I intend to lose every cent. I will give each copy to someone for free. Three years of writing cut down to 96 pages, folded over and staple-bound — I almost cried when the cover art came back grainier than I'd hoped for. I have only two boxes left, which means I've given away almost six hundred books in one year, which feels like a real accomplishment. My free book concept is a hard one to sell people on. You'd be surprised. Bookstores, in particular, don't react well. "We're a book*store*. We *sell* books." So I leave them in bars and laundromats, and in the record store my friend Craig opened with money from the time he was hit by a car.

I've left books on train cars in London, on street corners in Reykjavik, Iceland and Kansas City, Missouri, hoping they're passed on, that my stories travel further than I can myself. A free book is easy to pass on because you've made no investment. No reason to read it and then place it on your shelf like a trophy, because it has no aesthetic value. It doesn't even have a spine. A free book is my dad playing guitar at the flea market in Science Hill, Kentucky. It's my growing collection of CDs students hand me from their bands, handwritten fliers for Sunday afternoon shows in their parents' basements. It feels bad not to be legitimately published, but it feels good to control every aspect, from content to cover design to the 6x9 manila envelopes I use to mail them to people.

I even get letters back sometimes, or postcards that say, "Hey, I found your book in a Burger King bathroom in Salt Lake City." That never happened with the article I wrote for *Composition Studies*. In fact, I have no doubt that more people are reading the stuff that I photocopy and leave places for free. Would it feel good to have somebody else publish it, though? It would. It would feel good to have it in libraries. When I was a kid I used to dream about writing a book people could find in libraries. Burger King bathrooms never really entered those daydreams.

But the word is spreading, somehow. One person finds my book and tells someone else about it and they send me three stamps so I can mail them their own copy. Today I hit the post office to send off my two mail orders — one from Japan! I drop books in coffeehouses, the youth cultural center, in used clothing and record stores along Bardstown Road. In front of Craig's Records, a guy at the stoplight thinks he knows me from somewhere. "Hey!" he yells. "Hey man!"

I walk closer and squint into his car. "Do I know you?"

"Yeah, man. It's me, Jerry." He's frustrated that I still look confused. "*Jerry* ... the party guy?"

After I think about it, I am certain that this guy, Jerry the Party

Guy, was mistaken. I couldn't have met him because I really don't go to parties. I spent almost three straight years of my life writing at 10 PM every night, for one hour or three good pages, whichever came last, and that I would avoid planning anything that might interfere with that schedule. I wouldn't leave the apartment after eight just in case something drew my attention away from writing. I stopped having friends over because it was awkward to tell them to wait in the living room while I shut myself in the bedroom and wrote. I talk about keeping things moving, but while I was writing about movement a general sameness took over and I became grudgingly comfortable with it.

So even without a full-time job, I had a routine. I may be able to only go so far giving away free books, but I haven't stopped writing. There has to be a way I can do all of this at once. Choosing a career and accepting a full-time job shouldn't have to mean giving up variety, or giving up anything, really. It comes down to how I define myself. Am I a Full-time Lecturer or a failed ice cream man? Ed Minton the mechanic? Jerry the party guy? I don't want to be a writing instructor who's given up writing and gotten burned out from teaching the same syllabus year after year, giving the same paper assignments and writing the same rubber-stamp comments in the margins. "Tense confusion." "Is this your thesis?"

I don't want to be a teacher who wanted to be a writer. That's going to ruin both of them for me. I don't want to be like my dad who ran a garage but had no time left to work on his own cars. This is something to worry about.

Taking these low-commitment teaching jobs was a way to feel like I wasn't letting work take over my life, but I did put a lot of work into them. When I was a student, it seemed like professors had the easiest job in the world. They came in for a few classes a week, just like I did, but they got paid for it. Most of them seemed at least vaguely wealthy, and I had this idea that they spent the rest of their time at home reading books they liked, smoking pipes and listening to classical music. But now that I've seen this profession from the other side, I understand that I didn't see the whole picture.

Salaries in higher education, even for the actual professors, have not risen at the same rate as the money made by lawyers and doctors, or anything else that requires you to go to so many years of college. Plenty of people go all the way through five to seven years of a PhD program only to find that there aren't jobs available. Why aren't professors making more money? Why are they having such a hard time finding jobs straight out of graduate school? Because schools can hire people like me so much cheaper. In a lot of English departments, part-timers teach over sixty percent of the classes offered. That makes full-time, tenure-track positions scarce, which in turn drives the salaries down, because 300 people applied for this position and you should be thankful that you even found a job.

Now start paying us back those student loans.

So why do people do it? Prestige? Because after spending so much time in school, nothing else comes to mind? Because it seems easy? As far as the work itself, there are harder jobs out there. I won't lie to you; teaching can be a really easy job if you don't take it seriously. And some people don't, but I know way more professors and lecturers who work longer hours than they have to.

I come home exhausted from teaching. Not dirty and exhausted the way I did when I stocked shelves in a supermarket, but more like defeated and exhausted. The kind of exhaustion that taking a shower and watching late night television won't solve. I never left that supermarket saying, man, I could have stocked those shelves so much better. It just didn't go as I planned. I worked all last night to come up with a way to get those cans of creamed corn to line up, but they just didn't seem to get it.

But I also never left the supermarket saying, man, look at the way I just stocked those fucking shelves! Those customers are never going to look at canned peas the same way again.

Teaching doesn't feel like stocking shelves or bringing people their appetizers. It feels more like I'm creating something. It feels more like writing.

So I find a payphone. I call. I take the job. I will find a way to be a Full-time Lecturer and still be who I was before.

❊❊❊

Back at Minton's Auto, the Weather Channel announces a severe weather bulletin and displays a giant map of the Louisville area. Minton, Jr. gets all excited and says "Look Daddy, it's headed right for our house!"

While his son describes my engine trouble to me, I watch diabetic

Mr. Minton carefully unwrap his sack lunch and peel open an orange. As soon as he bites into it, he makes a face and spits into the garbage can. "I love oranges," he announces. "But that sumbitch was sour!"

Four

April 3, 2001
Digital Underground Plays Coyote's in Louisville

"The Humpty Dance. It's your chance. To do the Hump." The crowd is sweaty. A guy beside me is dancing for all he's worth, has been since an hour before the show. He must have hit his stride at some point and his body has gotten used to the dancing, because the sweat that covers his arms is cold. He feels like a hot dog just out of the package. I am pinned from the left by this hot-dog arm, and from the right by an older, mouthwash-smelling guy who smiles a lot and reminds me of my elementary school bus driver. By the end of the night, he will be dragged across the floor in a headlock for making fun of somebody's hat.

I am as excited to see Digital Underground tonight as I would have been when I was thirteen years old. Danielle and I arrive two hours early and claim our spot right in front of the stage. I tell her how lucky we are to witness this renewed interest in rap of the early 90's. It's true. Over the past two years, I've been able to see all the artists I missed at the peak of their talent because I was too young to get into clubs and had no transportation out of Eubank, Kentucky to larger, more urban areas. 2 Live Crew, Sir Mixalot, and now Digital Underground, all performing right here at Coyote's, a country line-dancing bar with cactuses painted on the walls and a saddle hanging from the ceiling, transformed with reflective plates into a shiny Western disco saddle.

Before the show, people dance on a fenced-in wooden floor. It looks like they've been corralled. Local radio DJs play records and toss beer koozies and bumper stickers to the crowd. "Who plays the hottest hip-hop in the 'Ville?"

"Hot 104," we say. We want the koozies.

The DJs play a new single from Petey Pablo, who urges us, "Take your shirt off, spin it like a helicopter." Two guys behind us take off their t-shirts and stomp around swinging them over their heads until a security guard says they have to put them back on.

"Mickey!" On my way to get drinks, I'm spotted by one of my students. This has happened before. After three and a half years of teaching as many classes as I can find, I've taught a good percentage of the people in Kentucky and Indiana. I have some history with Jason. He's in my W290, Advanced College Writing class this semester, but before that he took Intro with me. He wrote about moving to the desert after high school and working for two years as an apprentice to a glass-blower, about seeing someone get hit by a car at the last-ever Grateful Dead concert. Every student at IUS has to take Intro to Writing, but Jason was one of the few students who actually wanted to be a writer. "A travel writer, maybe, or do something like Hunter S. Thompson." In W290 I'm supposed to teach him how to take his energy and channel it through academics.

Jason has an amazing energy for writing, but it's short-lived. He enrolls in college one semester at a time, leaving for new adventures when he gets tired of studying. I haven't seen him in over a week.

"So you listen to Digital Underground?"

"For almost half my life." I realized on my birthday last year, listening to my old CDs, that most of them were released over a decade ago. Some of my favorites I still have on cassette, dubbed on cheap Memorex by friends I've lost track of. But Geto Boys, Bass Boy — I still have the tapes. "Have you met Danielle?"

"Yeah, you introduced us last semester. This is my friend Amy." Amy half-waves and then walks off. "What are you two drinking?" Jason sells pieces of his glass art for as much as seven hundred dollars. He wants to buy me a beer. "Man, I was here last time DU played. After the show they invited everybody to follow them to that strip club across the street ... they got *freaky*." He asks Danielle and me to join him at his table, and I sit down with a careful eye on my spot by the stage.

Then begin the questions. "So this paper that's due on Monday is a first draft, right?"

"Um, yeah."

"And how many sources do we need?"

"Well," I say, "it's not so much the number of them you need to worry about. I mean, the whole thing should be based on your ideas, what *you* have to say. First just sit down and brainstorm this paper the way you'd write it if you didn't even need outside research. Then go back and see how your ideas fit in with other people." Danielle's bored, drawing shapes with her fingernail in the frost on her glass. "You remember how we talked about joining the conversation?" Jason doesn't remember.

"Think of it this way," I tell him. "You see that group of guys by the restroom?"

"With the trench coats?"

"Yeah. Well, you wouldn't walk right up to them and just start talking about whatever was on your mind, right?"

"No, they look pretty fuckin' hardcore."

"Research is kind of like that. You have to find out where the conversation stands and then see where you can fit into it, how you have something new to add to it, something interesting to say." I almost get lost in the words. I believe them, but they feel hollow tonight, like I'm reading them straight off the syllabus. Like I'm not even listening to myself.

"Guess I'm staying up late tonight."

Behind us a Bud girl is dancing in place with her arms stiff, looking unsure of herself, confined to her tiny island, a platform where she keeps watch over a tub full of ice and beer. More drinks are delivered to our table by Brandi, a student from two years ago. "Who had the Maker's and Coke?" I'm staring at her — can't remember her name for a few seconds, and neurons are firing in my brain, trying to put her face into context — which school, which semester? But she places me first — "Hey! You were my teacher!" I feel awful about it and will leave her a huge tip. Brandi's taking some time off from school, she tells us. "This isn't bad for a part-time job but I don't make enough to cover tuition."

I offer to pay for this second round, but Jason waves me off with a wad of dollars. Brandi moves on to new tables and Jason turns the conversation back to his paper. "Well, I'll get something written this weekend. I just have to figure out what the hell I'm trying to say with it." His eyes narrow — he's thinking, putting his ideas together. "I know I'm getting a late start," he admits. "I saw you walking on Bardstown Road the other night, and I was gonna roll down my window and yell at you, but then I figured you're off-duty. I know I wouldn't want people asking me questions about work."

He's right. Normally it doesn't bother me, but right now the last thing I want to talk about is Jason's paper. Like when we used to scam free haircuts from Danielle's hairdresser uncle — I never understood why he grumbled under his breath those Friday nights, or pressed a little too hard with the clippers. But now I'm exhausted. I've been talking about writing since nine this morning: two classes, a department meeting, and putting together a presentation for this weekend in Maryland. So all I can offer Jason tonight are these stock responses, my own vague theories about writing in general instead of anything specific to the paper he's working on. My writing advice used to sound so honest, so natural, until I started repeating it. Teaching classes back to back, offering the same advice one hour to the next has cheapened what I have to say. Now it sounds no better than a textbook.

I try to force myself to say something more original, something just for Jason, but it isn't there tonight. I want to tell him to forget the paper, stay up all night drinking and hanging out with Digital Underground. Instead, though, I change the topic of conversation — "So what other rap shows have you been to?" Jason and Danielle discuss hip-hop performance styles and I glance back at Brandi passing out Jell-O shots. Did she learn anything useful in my class? Was she at least able to have some fun with writing? Or was it all just a requirement, just a letter grade on a transcript, the way I felt about math classes when I was a student. I know that when we leave tonight I won't see Jason on Monday morning. In my mailbox I'll find his rough two pages of ideas for the assignment, and that will be the last I'll hear from him. When the lights go down in the club, the three of us stand up to go separate directions — Danielle and me to the front of the stage, and Jason to a table of Bud girls he notices in the back.

❊ ❊ ❊

The spotlights come up and focus on the stage's backdrop — a mural of the desert at nightfall, complete with tumbleweeds and a howling coyote with a bandana around its neck. The Get Down Family plays first —, gritty Louisville hip-hop. It's chaos. There are twenty people on stage, most of them there for encouragement, to get the crowd and the MCs hyped up. One member's job is to walk from one end of the stage to the other with a giant flag that says "Get Down Family." The crowd really gets into it.

Then Digital Underground hits the stage hard with *Doowhutchyalike*. "Now *as* the record spins around, you recognize this sound. Well it's the Underground. We came to get down with *whutchyalike*. With what ya like." The sample kicks in two seconds before they

34

jump on stage, and their feet hit the ground with the first two words. We're sprayed with malt liquor and silly string and I feel this disbelief, like I've been waiting my whole life for this. I remember when I was a kid they played in Nashville, and even though I had no better chance of going to that concert than any other one on their tour, it was that much more disappointing because it was so close. So close.

There are shows I have missed that I can never let go — ones I couldn't afford or that happened too far away from me. And I regret it for years. I've always known that with Digital Underground in particular that I really missed something, and now I see what it was. DU comes out with insane energy and they keep the momentum, popping through five songs non-pause before Shock-G decides to slow things down a little. He moves back to his keyboard and gives us a medley of hooks from radio hits before he comes back to center stage to play "Same Song," the first record that Tupac Shakur ever rhymed on. When they come to Tupac's verse, Shock-G holds the mic to the crowd and everyone yells his part. Tupac was a member of Digital Underground when he was nineteen, before he sold double platinum, before he went to jail, before he was shot and killed in Las Vegas.

Same Song leads into a Tupac tribute. The spotlights go down. People hold up their lighters and Shock-G offers a few brief words. "Get your lighters up for all the talented brothers we keep losing. Tupac, Biggie, Big Pun, Big L, Eazy E, Freaky Tah, Kurt Cobain . . ." He rhymes through two verses of Tupac's "Hail Mary," one of his friend's darkest songs, then stands with his eyes closed, microphone down. Hip-hop shows have become somber over the past few years.

But Shock-G knows how to incorporate these moments without losing momentum. "A lot of talented brothers keep dying, and we owe them a moment of silence. But there are a lot of talented brothers from Oakland still alive, and let's give them a moment of motherfucking *noise* — The Luniz!" These absolute surprise guests rush onstage with almost as much energy as the Underground. Danielle is jumping, smiling, singing along. This appearance is so unexpected that we don't even notice Shock-G slip off the stage. But as The Luniz end their one song, Shock-G reappears as MC Humpty Hump, wearing his Groucho Marx glasses with the black nose to match his skin tone, a feather headdress and a leopard-print miniskirt.

Shock-G and Humpty Hump are two clearly different personas. Played by the same person, but with totally different voices and performance styles. Humpty is as goofy as Shock-G is smooth. Listening to the album, you wouldn't even know it was the same person behind both voices. That was part of the whole excitement for me tonight, to see how they'd pull it off on stage, like when you're a kid and you know it's your cousin Jeff who sneaks off from dinner to dress up as Santa Claus, but you still want to see him in the costume. Shock-G had been all over the stage as himself, but Humpty Hump comes out with ten times that energy, jumping around so much that he can barely finish his verses:

> ... but sometimes I get ridiculous
> I'll eat up all your crackers and your licorice
> Hey yo, fat girl! C'mere, are you ticklish?

> Yes ladies, I'm really bein' sincere
> Cause in a 69 my Humpty nose will tickle your rear

When I was too young to understand what a 69 was I used to think he said "tickle your ear." I never understood why they censored it in the video.

> Black people, do the Humpty Hump
> White people, do the Humpty Hump
> Puerto Ricans, do the Humpty Hump
> Samoans, do the Humpty Hump

The Humpty Dance is all-inclusive. At one point Humpty brings up people from the crowd who want to put their own rhyming skills to the test. He creates an impromptu freestyle competition. People get four lines apiece and then they have to pass the mic. As the microphone comes to each participant, the DJ changes up the beat and tempo, sometimes classic breakbeats, sometimes something thrown together on the spot. People are eliminated one-by-one based on audience reaction.

Winners are declared and Humpty invites new people to the stage — "All the freaky ladies come up and we'll play 'Freaks of the Industry.'" Women are pushing past me from all directions, trying to get noticed by the band. Boyfriends hold them up, boost the closer ones onto the stage so they can be chosen by Digital Underground. Danielle cowers behind me. Halfway through the song, I can't even see the band members. The entire stage is full of Louisville's freakiest ladies getting freaky. We spot Jason's friend Amy, now very drunk, humping Humpty so hard that he has to pry her off.

As a final song, Humpty wants to do *Doowutchyalike* again. *"Please.*

It's my *favorite* Digital Underground song, and I wasn't out here when they played it before." After eleven years or more, Digital Underground throws this much energy into their show, and they still love it themselves. They're out on the road every night, playing frat houses and country bars. When I saw Sir Mixalot play Coyote's, he looked tired, looked like he was touring out of some obligation. He played his early hits because it was expected, not because hearing them still makes him shake with excitement. I see longstanding favorite bands play shows like an uncle who's tired of telling the same jokes every Thanksgiving, no matter how much you still ask to hear them. But Digital Underground, they're out here for fun, which makes me happier than I can even explain.

After the show I try to buy a CD from one of the opening bands. Their DJ tells me I can get one from his bandmate, who's busy focusing a handheld video camera on a blond girl by the edge of the stage, trying to get her to lift up her shirt. The bouncers nod their approval and he steadily videotapes for fifteen minutes while I stand there in the side of the frame, money in hand, looking uncomfortable. This girl is gyrating and rubbing her huge fake breasts and I'm looking back and forth from the ceiling to the floor, checking my watch. Eventually, I give up and walk away.

On the ride home in the car, Danielle and I get into an argument about underground hip hop and whether it should have some kind of idealism behind it that sets it apart from major-label top 40 rap. I tell her she's trying to apply punk rock ethics to a totally different music and she asks me what's the use of doing something different musically if you're going to fall into the same excesses and downfalls that the stuff on the radio does — in other words, why set yourself apart artistically if you're going to be just as sexist?° We get really pissed off at each other.

✵ ✵ ✵

April 4, 2001
Conference on Constructing Cyberculture(s): Performance, Pedagogy and Politics in Online Spaces. College Park, Maryland

---

° Looking back, her argument makes a lot more sense than mine. I'm not really sure what I was defending. The right to look at huge fake breasts if you want to?

*Through their homepages, university faculty members can negoti-
ate personal representation within a professional space, and can
move toward a wholeness that designates Marx's unalienated worker. Bruce Horner notes in his introduction to* Terms of Work for
Composition: A Materialist Critique *(2000) that "work"
denotes "simultaneously an activity, the product of that activity,
and the place of its practice" (p. xvii). Each aspect of this definition
plays a role in the way faculty construct identity online. My paper
examines the ways faculty members can use their homepages to
represent the personal alongside the professional, and to reclaim
parts of their identities that can be lost within their role as workers.
(Hess, 2000)*

At the Amtrak station outside Baltimore, there is a young man
about my age practicing Tai Chi. He has developed such concentration
and precision for it that he stands without moving, literally on the edge
of the platform, two feet from the trains that speed past him. His hands
meet in a triangle, his body extends at a 45-degree angle toward the
platform, and I watch him hold this position for twenty minutes. People
in the glass walkway that brings them over the track from the ticket-
purchasing area stop and stare, each one of them questioning if this Tai
Chi figure is a statue instead of a person.

Danielle and I aren't taking the Amtrak itself, but a cheaper, slower commuter train that should take us from the airport to somewhere
near our hotel. After buying our tickets, we talk to Sean, a college
freshman from Indianapolis, in town for a fraternity convention. He's
one of those people who form a personality out of being clearly
impressed or surprised with everything. "Those trains are *fast!*" he tells
us. "That guy is standing *still.*" He's never heard of Digital
Underground.

The wind on the platform is cold and I have to hold down loose
sheets from my conference program with every finger and the businessman one bench down from ours struggles with the paper wrapping of his
Quarter Pounder with Cheese. I'm making last-minute revisions to my
presentation — "A Nomad Faculty: English Professors' Online
Representations of Work, Product, and Workplace." I get travel reim-
bursement and a special laminated nametag. Sean nods at the nametag.
"You here for the conference at Georgetown?"

"University of Maryland."

"Is that in DC?"

"Nope. College Park."

"That's a lonnnng train ride."

We stare together at the Tai Chi person, who is now holding a new position. Sean raises his eyebrows. "I gotta get some food," he says with his eyes wide. "Then I'm gonna take me a nap, but first off I gotta get some food. That fat guy's cheeseburger looks *good*."

❈ ❈ ❈

At the conference, there's a long wooden table full of cheese cubes, fruit, and the same stale wheat crackers they have at all these academic events. The spread is set up way too far in advance and since I don't wake up in time for the early sessions, the cheese is now sort of warm and glossed-over and it sticks to my fingers. I take some anyway because it's free, and don't want to put it back on the tray in case someone has already seen me touch it. Danielle picks up two fruit cups for us — they're heavy on the maraschino cherries and smell suspiciously like kerosene.

My session is scheduled for 1:30. I'm presenting directly before Jill Arnold, a psychology professor from Nottingham-Trent University and one of the main researchers I cite in my paper. She researches the internet homepages of professors, a subject that is surprisingly interesting. A lot of professors, for instance, like to post pictures of themselves whitewater rafting, maybe to offset the fact that they spend so much time sitting at their desks adding pictures to their webpages.

The best thing about this Cybercultures conference is how people have connected the topic of technology to all sorts of stuff. Just looking through the program, every paper is so different from the one before it:

"African American Quilters and Internet Usage"
— *Kyra Hicks, University of Maryland*

"'No One Does Sex Like a Pro': Prostitutes, Political Action and The Internet"
— *Lara Pullen, University of Wisconsin*

"The Pop Culturalization of U.S. Politics on the Net: A Counterintuitive Model of Irresponsible Journalism for the Possibility of A Reborn Democracy"
— *Paul Mackie, Georgetown University*

"Cyber Cherry Blossoms: Mail Order Brides and the
Construction of the Virtual Filipina"
— *L. Clare Bratten, Middle Tennessee State*

All day, though, as interesting as some of the presentations are, something seems off about them. They seem a little dry after the Digital
Underground show. Nobody brings in any theatrics — they just walk up
to the podium, maybe start off with an uncomfortable joke, and recite
their papers. Not that I did anything spectacular myself. Maybe at the
next conference, I'll switch nametags halfway through my presentation.
— put on a blonde plastic wig and become "Uncle Flexible — Neptune
University," deliver the rest of the paper in a villainous accent. Imagine
if I had something interesting to say? All these academics would cite me.
"As argued by Uncle Flexible (2001), the homepages of English professors reveal a struggle between institutional and personal control of identity."

One thing rappers and academics do have in common is that they
love to cite each other. Seriously. Listen to a hip hop album. "Like Rakim
said, I wanna move the crowd ..." (LL Cool J, 1991). "I got the phuncky
feel like B-Real" (Defari, 1999). Uncle Flexible would refer to both, pit-
ting rappers and academics against each other. His half of the presentation would be conducted in battle rhymes. It's not like he wouldn't have
anything serious to say — his presentation would be pretty much along
the lines of mine, but there'd be more breakdancing incorporated. A *lot*
more breakdancing. People don't do it very often. You'd be surprised.

❀ ❀ ❀

The University of Maryland alumni center is all high ceilings and
marble columns. Each person from the conference gets a ticket for one
free drink, and most of us wander around the front lobby like nametag
zombies, holding thin paper napkins underneath our glasses and introducing ourselves to other people who study whatever obscure topic
we've chosen to spend our time writing about. Some of these conferences can get pretty stuffy (if you can believe that). But Cybercultures
hasn't been around long enough to earn that much prestige, so there is
actually a good balance between older, established academics and
younger people still surprised they were even invited. After our social
obligations to the conference dinner are fulfilled, the people who live in
the area take the rest of us into DC. Danielle and I follow three other
conference people onto the Metro:

Mindy: grad student from Georgetown University. Here to present a paper about ultimate Frisbee chat rooms.

Jocelyn: works at the Pentagon. Here to talk about altruism online.

Dan: "Securing Funding For Your Technology Project: Selling Your Ideas (Without Including Your Soul)." Another Georgetown grad student. Teaches high school somewhere in Virginia.

Carl: women's studies instructor from Reno, Nevada. His paper is on images of women in video games — "Big Guns, Sexist Games, Radical Pleasure: Grrlz Frag Gender Online."

Video games, ultimate Frisbee ... we make these connections between our real life interests and academic credibility. I'm the nerd of the group looking at professors on the web, but now I want to write about Digital Underground and secret identities. I want to write about how Vanilla Ice changed what it meant to be white and involved in hip hop. I have some ideas, I think.

From our Metro stop in DC, Mindy and Jocelyn take us to hear jazz at HR-57. I ask half-seriously if the club is named after HR of Bad Brains, and no one has heard of him.° Danielle and I spend the next twenty minutes trying to give these DC-residents some sense of the importance and influence of their punk scene. This club didn't have a liquor license, so their set-up works this way: you bring in your own drinks in a black garbage bag, pay them two dollars per person, like a transporting fee. There are empty bottles on our table from previous drinkers. The jazz is improvisational — musicians move to the stage, jumping into the rhythm, no one stepping on anyone's toes to show off or become the focus. Carl tells a story about living in Ireland. Dan knows the saxophone player.

See? At night we take off our masks. The last conference I went to, in Kansas City, it depressed me watching professors who have been in it too long drinking at the hotel bar, making jokes that reference Derrida or Foucault. But we're not like them tonight. Seriously. We

---

*The club is actually named after a 1987 House Resolution that proclaimed jazz "a rare and valuable national American treasure."

can play the role, but we can turn it off anytime we want. With them it was sad, but for us it's vital, every drink bringing us closer to our true selves behind these academic masks. Until the end of the night when it becomes sad again. Dan looks older drunk. Outside the club we're leaving, saying goodbye, walking back toward Mindy's apartment, leaving Dan to catch a cab home to Virginia. I see creases in his face that weren't there before, and his eyes look defeated.

4 AM, hands in our pockets, we're hopping across sidewalks onto front stoops, waking up Mindy's neighbors. Mindy has offered to let us sleep in her apartment, since Carl and Danielle and I missed the last Metro back to College Park hours ago. Carl says something about Post-Georgian architecture in this part of the city and he and Mindy debate the features that distinguish Georgian from *Post*-Georgian. I watch a bug disappear into a crack in the sidewalk. Carl gets excited and laughs like we're still in the jazz club. Lights come on in kitchen windows and Mindy rushes us inside.

Her couch folds out for Danielle and me, and there's an extra bed downstairs for Carl. I try to teach them how to play Settlers of Catan. It's a sort of naturalist-Monopoly board game Mindy's roommate has — I have it at home. But they find it hard to pay attention. Carl is especially hyper. You play the game by settling the island of Catan and developing resources to trade with the other players. Different climates produce lumber, ore, brick, or sheep. Carl kept holding up his sheep cards and making baa noises. Soon we give up and go to bed. Mindy brings us an extra blanket and shows Carl downstairs to his spot. I fall asleep to him hopping up and down at the foot of the narrow, winding staircase, telling some convoluted story. I wake up periodically during the next two hours, and every time Carl is still talking, talking.[°]

I hear him leave around 7 to put finishing touches on his presentation. Danielle and I get up to borrow a map from Mindy's Yellow Pages so we can check out some of the monuments before we take the Metro back to see Carl's presentation. He follows a session called "Virtual Vaginas and Pentium Penises: A Critical Study of Teledildonics and Digital Stimulation." He switches the projector's display from dildos of the future to his screenshots from classic video games. He talks about representations of women — how they're either turned into prizes like the princesses in *Super Mario Brothers* or *Legend of Zelda*, or completely sexualized like in *Tomb Raider*. Three

---

[°]Danielle says that at some point she remembers him talking about elephants.

audience members know he finished it a few hours ago, probably still drunk, but he pulls it off. It sounds spontaneous, but authoritative, like he might really know what he's talking about (Carl, 2001).

Five

There are books in which big-time university professors take a paid sabbatical to work at a series of blue collar jobs so they can write about the struggles of the working class and see how the other half lives. What those professors seem to ignore is that two floors down, in the basements of their own buildings, there are plenty of people working paycheck to paycheck for colleges, waiting tables on the weekends, and teaching the classes left unstaffed when the professors went on sabbatical to write books about the plight of the worker.

College tuition is getting higher and higher, but more and more courses are being taught by low-paid adjuncts. There's something wrong with a system that trains people to do nothing but train more people. The cycle has to end somewhere. Do I think part-time college instructors are the most exploited workers out there? No. But I do think that people still enter college with the promise of more earning potential, and that they don't necessarily come out with that anymore. And when universities graduate students and then hire them back, cheap, to teach new students, it starts to look like a problem. It starts to look like a scam.

But the exploitation goes both ways. I have to admit that being just out of college myself, there was something reassuring about still being there.

Everyone I knew in college works there now. My friend Jake, who believed I was stealing an ice cream truck, is an academic advisor. His wife, Carrie, is an administrative assistant who dreams of becoming a librarian. Jake, like me, came to college planning to do something that made some money. He was torn between majoring in law and international business with a minor in Japanese. We were both lucky enough to have girlfriends who talked us out of these plans, and these girlfriends became our wives. When Danielle and I were in college, Jake and Carrie were the only other people our age that we knew who were married.

We met Jake when he was night manager at Craig's Records. Jake needed a ride home. Danielle and I wanted some free CDs. So we struck a deal. We drove him home, he invited us in and introduced us to Carrie and then fell instantly asleep on the couch. What we wouldn't have guessed about Jake was that he loved to work. Carrie told us he was working fifty hours a week on top of his full-time college classes. He worked mornings at McDonald's and nights at the record store. His exhaustion left Carrie alone to entertain Danielle and me, two strangers Jake brought home by surprise. We offered to leave them alone for the night, but Carrie wanted to cook cream of potato soup. She was bored and not sleepy yet. So the three of us bonded by putting makeup on Jake while he snored.

So back then, Jake worked at McDonald's and the record store. Carrie worked at Target. Danielle and I didn't do anything. We were still sticking to our plan to take out as many student loans as possible and pay our future selves back when we made more money. My scheme had even taken on a new scope: I wasn't going to pay back the loans.

I spent four years living off student loans, which sounds like a bad idea in the long-term, but let me explain. Here's what I was thinking at the time: Unless you grew up wealthy, the whole idea of college is basically financial. Investing in your own future and all that. Like I said before, when I was in college I considered student loans free money to be paid back by my 22-year-old self, the guy with the degree and the job, or the guy who learned so much about writing in college that he's able to make a living at it (at that time I believed people could still make a living from something like writing books).

I didn't know this guy who was my future self, so I was fucking him over like I might fuck over a stranger. But this guy was also me, and I couldn't expect myself to change to a nose-to-the-grindstone asshole in the span of four years. I couldn't expect this future self to think that different from me. So I studied the fine print of the student loan booklet. I found a loophole. I had a back-up plan.

Phase One: for students enrolled at least half-time, student loan payments are deferred. Your payments resume after a six-month grace period when you stop taking classes. So if I stayed in school half-time half the year, taking six hours every other semester, I would in fact *never* have to pay back my loans.

Phase Two: professors get free tuition. Use student loans to pay for

46

enough classes to become a professor. Sign up for my own classes for free, and flunk myself every semester. Why flunk myself? Ethics.

Am I doing this? No. I have resigned myself to my Sallie Mae payment. Saving the money is not worth the effort. Sometimes, today, I look at myself and I think I've been trapped by my own schemes, that all that avoiding work became work in itself, work leading to more work. Those plans and that future that stretched out before me lasted a few months after college, in different variations, and then my future life kind of collapsed onto the present me.

I didn't feel this way about work before I met Danielle. She was a huge influence on me, and the more time Jake spent with us, the more his work ethic deteriorated too. Jake loved the record store, even loved McDonald's, but within a few months Carrie quit her job at Target, Jake quit both his jobs, and they took out student loans. The rest of us had given Jake shit for working too hard, but for a year after that he did nothing — he was void of ambition. It was depressing. I felt guilty.

I can't explain how this dynamic developed of Jake being the butt of our jokes. He could easily crush me, but when we play basketball he's the one who ends up on the pavement, holding his ankle. He's the one who got hurt when we tried to play tennis blindfolded. He's injury-prone, and he doesn't take himself too seriously. Most of the stories I could tell about Jake end with him wearing a dress that's made for a five-foot woman instead of a six-foot man, or with Carrie driving him to the hospital. Sometimes both at once.

Jake and Carrie introduced us to Will and Lara, who have university jobs too. Will works in the Honors College, and his girlfriend Lara works with Jake in the advising office. Will is the same height as Carrie. Lara is the same height as Jake. Will and I share an interest in the computer graphics program Adobe Photoshop. We scanned in pictures from Jake's family photo albums and created a website as a surprise for Jake's birthday. In one picture we replaced everyone else's head with Jake's, so that there are seven or eight of him posing in front of a Christmas tree. In another one, we spliced in a naked guy next to his mom on the couch.

Lara plays guitar in a jazz ensemble. Will enjoys not liking things. Here is a short list of things he does not like:

Pancakes — "They're too sweet. With syrup at least. Sometimes I'll eat one with a good strawberry preserve."

47

Ice cream — "I don't like it. I like ice *milk*."

Watermelon — "Too messy. I don't like the seeds. I haven't eaten it since I was eleven."

Kids at the bus stop ask Will if he's Harry Potter. This frustrates him, and frustrated he looks even more cartoonish. At the comic book store, he buys action figures that can pass for tiny likenesses. Danielle and I put them into strange poses at his apartment — Will-on-Will action. Lara and Will are getting married next year. They keep their money in separate bank accounts and plan to always do so.

❧ ❧ ❧

This question of money is a bigger one recently, now that I have student loan payments and Danielle is graduating into her own six-month grace period before the bills start to come. When we were twenty-year-old newlyweds, Danielle made it fun not to have any money. She somehow created a hobby out of something that had made me miserable for far too many of the first nineteen years of my life. Our time together meant much more to us than buying CDs or washing our clothes at the laundromat, so we ate at Taco Bell most nights and wore our clothes until we spilled something on them.

I went from being a kid who yelled at his parents for not having more money to a man who valued nothing more than his free time. I went from being a kid who kept a secret shoebox full of money he never spent to a college student who was proud to steal toilet paper from the apartment complex laundry room. Nothing was worth more to me than time spent with Danielle, and having no money had become an adventure. When my mom and I talked about my change in outlook, she remembered feeling that way too when she got married. "It gets much less fun once you have kids," she said. I couldn't tell if she was criticizing me for all the complaining I used to do or just trying to make me think, but either way I can see what she's talking about.

Danielle and I don't have kids, but we do have the cats and the iguana to take care of. We spend most of our money on vet bills. Allergy shots, punctured toes, eye injuries. It's like it's never-ending. They know my name in the 24-hour emergency room at the animal hospital. I had to rush Semphonius, our youngest cat, to the hospital because one of his pupils was three times the size of the other one. They thought he was having a stroke, but it turned out to be an infection caused by a scratch from our other cat. The vet prescribed some kind of expensive gel we have to massage into his

48

eye three times a day.

One of the cats snagged Decimus' toe and we had to rush her to the vet too. I never knew an iguana could bleed so much. She didn't eat for almost a week afterward — we offered her everything: collard greens, broccoli, carrots, bananas, tangerines, but she wouldn't touch any of it until Danielle remembered reading that iguanas can eat tofu. And they can. It was like Decimus had been waiting her whole life to eat tofu. She ate an entire block that night and wouldn't touch any other kind of food for the next two months. Finally we had to take her back to the vet because she was getting too aggressive — her protein levels were elevated from eating too much tofu.

Decimus is our middle child, and our only reptile. No cage can contain her, so she has her own room, and has chased each of the cats out of this room at some point, although we try to keep the door shut. When our friends housesit, we bombard them with Post-it notes, written as if they were reminders from our animals themselves — "Please remember to carefully close my door. It catches — Decimus the Emperor." "Don't feed me whip-cream, no matter how much I may beg. It is bad for me — Semphonius Gracchus." "Make sure I eat my own food, and do not steal from Semphonius, as I am prone to do — Black Ulysses." Our pets have full names, at Danielle's insistence.

The younger cat, Semphonius, is recovering from an addiction to aerosol whip-cream. It was bad. He knew the sound of the can and if anything brushed against it, if it rattled at all, he came running. He's a long-haired cat and the tufts on the bottoms of his feet are a dangerous combination with slick hardwood floors. Blackie is two years older than Semphonius, and technically his aunt, I think. I should ask Will to use his knowledge of genealogy to trace back the family tree of cats my parents have owned. Blackie was my dad's cat originally. He named her, and used to let her drink whiskey with him in his garage, where she lived for the first year of her life, until the paint fumes forced her outside, where the ragweed took its toll on her allergies. She's allergic to the outdoors. She's allergic to fleas. Basically, she's allergic to being a cat.

For the past three years we've been dealing with Blackie's Feline Immunodeficiency Virus (FIV), the feline version of HIV. When we first got her, her ribs were showing and she was missing fur on the back half of her body. Inside the apartment, though, she's fine, except for her aversion to the litter box. She scratches in the litter, climbs out of the box to shit on the floor, and then climbs back in to scratch in the litter. We can't break her of this habit. The FIV makes her susceptible to gum infections, so we have to take her in for blood tests and teeth cleanings every six months, and keep her separated from Semphonius so that he doesn't contract it too. It's been a tough decision. Do we keep them totally isolated from each other, which makes them miserable, or do we keep them together, which puts Semphonius at risk for a terminal disease? We compromise by watching them closely when we're at home, and separating them when we leave. Before we leave the apartment, we have to close Decimus in one bedroom, Semphonius in the other, and give Blackie free reign to destroy furniture throughout the rest of the house. We make everyone take their shoes off on the way in so that we don't track in dangerous germs for Blackie's weakened immune system.

With our apartment already turned over to animals, Danielle thought it made sense to apply for a job at the zoo. Somebody had to break the cycle. We can't all work at the same school forever.

I miss Danielle when she's at work. She's never worked somewhere that I couldn't walk across campus to eat lunch with her. But she calls me with updates, or to let me know that the peanut butter and pumpkin butter sandwich I made her was particularly good. The zoo job has its advantages, she says. "The people I work with are pretty cool, the hours aren't too long, and I can walk over and see the lemurs anytime I want." She loves the lemurs. On breaks she'll eat her peanut butter sandwich outside their habitat while she watches them, but the lemurs respond with strange, uncomfortable stares. They huddle, all the while glaring at her — even the ones called Social Ghosts — then they line up and walk back into their hiding spot out of view.

Some days I get to eat lunch with her if we can time it right. The zoo never tells her ahead of time when her breaks are or even what time she can leave. They wait and see how busy things are, how many people are buying tickets, and then they send people home arbitrarily, with no warning and no concern for who's been there since 9 AM or who got there two hours ago. They just walk over and tell you to leave. The schedule is distributed each Wednesday, but it only lists the time your shift begins, never what time you can go home. Danielle says there are even signs posted: "Remember: You know what time you come in, but not what time you will leave."

The whole place is full of signs, both professionally-printed and crude homemade ones taped to the walls, like "Don't touch my computer." There's some infighting between Admissions, where Danielle works, and the PhotoAmerica booth next door. From what Danielle heard of the story, the feud began last summer when PhotoAmerica borrowed a fan from Admissions and somehow broke it before it could be returned. Zoo management handled the dispute by making a new rule that no one from

Admissions can speak to anyone from PhotoAmerica.

Danielle sits in a tiny air-conditioned ticket box. People buy zoo tickets when it's already raining and then try to return them ten minutes later. All day, Danielle has to explain there are no refunds because it's an outdoor facility. "That's what I do — recite the no-refund policy and list prices to people who have spent the past five minutes holding up the line while they studied the prices on the wall behind me."

Benefits of the zoo job, though, include the gift shop discount, which Danielle uses to buy stuffed orangutans, a giant stuffed boa constrictor, and a stuffed Komodo dragon who becomes the girlfriend for our iguana. She also gets a seemingly endless number of free passes. The big attraction this summer is "Beauty and the Beast" — butterflies and Komodo dragons. The butterflies are housed in this huge indoor area, and it's the job of some unfortunate zoo worker to guard the opening and recite an instructional speech before each person goes in. I went in right behind a second grade class and heard the teacher translate perfectly clear English to her students:

> Now what the zoo lady said is that you *can't* touch the butterflies. You're *not allowed* to touch the butterflies. If you feel like you might touch the butterflies, put your hands in your pockets.

She said it like each word was punctuated with its own period.

I followed behind the group of kids. As soon as we walked in, I was face to face with Will Oldham just inside the door. He was wearing a baseball cap and staring straight up into the air.

Will Oldham is an esoteric figure, a balding Louisville indie musician with huge bushy sideburns, validated forever since Johnny Cash covered one of his songs. He was standing there in the middle of hundreds of fluttering exotic butterflies, not saying a word, not even blinking. It looked like he was part of the exhibit. Just past the exit I heard a mother ask her three-year-old to recap his day at the zoo. "Did you see the giraffes? Did you see the butterflies?"

"Did you see Will Oldham?" I wanted to ask.

The butterfly exhibit, for some reason, is a big topic of conversation this summer. Maybe because of Danielle's connection to the zoo, or people just naturally bring it up. And every time somebody does, I picture Will Oldham still standing there after they close up at night and all the lights go out, stationed just inside the door with his eyes open while the butterflies sleep.

✳ ✳ ✳

I'm paying more attention to how people spend their time. With Danielle at the zoo all day, and no real office for me to work in, I spend most of my day at home. I read papers and plan assignments and write stories. I work on publicity for the upcoming Icelandic poetry showcase I put together, and I go to meetings. A lot of them. There was one meeting to decide how many meetings we should have this semester. So when you put it all together, the bulk of my time is spent writing, or teaching writing, or thinking about writing. One of the older lecturers tells me that people reach intellectual maturity around twenty-five years of age, so it's unfair for us to expect students to have the same kind of drive and focus at eighteen. I can see what he's talking about. I've developed this work ethic lately, this desire to do a good job with the things I choose to participate in. It was one of those statements that sounded so good when I heard it. It seemed to explain so much until I talked to Carrie about it. "Maybe it's not intellectual maturity," she said. "Maybe at that point you give up on finding anything good to do."

We don't want to see each other change. We make fun of Jake when he buys polo shirts and tucks them into his khaki pants before going to work. We resent each other for becoming anything different than we have been, but we're all looking for something different. We're confused. We say we're against stagnation, but we pass up any chance to move out of Louisville. Each of us after graduating move directly into working at the same college we've attended for four or five years. We thought we were delaying the future, but sticking around here became just another way to be comfortable or settled, a way to complain about changes by not making any.

Six

In the past three months I have been an ice cream man and a college instructor. I have seen Digital Underground play in a cowboy bar and learned about the digitization of pleasure in a fancy hotel's multi-purpose room. I have driven back and forth between my Kentucky apartment and my new Indiana job approximately 96 times — I'm a full-fledged commuter now. I carry one of those travel mugs. I was so focused on everything that was happening that I had almost forgotten those copies of *El Cumpleanos de Paco* that I left in bars and laundromats around the world. And now my homemade book has been reviewed in an Icelandic newspaper.

My friend Michael calls to tell me. "Have you seen the Reykjavik morning news today?"

"Um, no."

"Well you're in it!"

Fuck yes. I couldn't get one review in a Louisville paper, but I am big in Scandinavia. If by big you mean two reviews. The first one was in some death metal magazine out of Finland, but this is *Morgunblad*, the morning newspaper of Reykjavik. Michael promises to translate it and mail it to me. "Did they like it?" I ask.

"Well ..." he says. "I'd call it forty percent positive." I think I can live with that.

I left copies of *Paco* in Reykjavik when Danielle and I went there for our fifth wedding anniversary. She had mentioned the idea years ago, when we had no idea how people made money, back when we were excited to find food stamps someone had dropped in the street. I taught an extra class specifically to save money for the trip and surprise her. I packed one hundred copies of *Paco* and dragged them around airports in a suitcase with a broken wheel. We spent four days in Iceland, and the trip went like this:

Reykjavik, Day One: We had some contacts when we hit the

ground — Michael and Bragi, two of the finest writers in Iceland — but I had forgotten to bring their phone numbers with me. My total confusion about the Icelandic phone book left Danielle and me to navigate the city ourselves that first night. We relied on our pirated travel guide — purchased from Barnes & Noble then returned for a refund after I photocopied the sections we needed — it was outdated but gave us a map of the city center along with a list of interesting bars and restaurants that had closed years ago. Danielle and I walked in circles, looking at Christmas lights and trying to compare street signs with the crude grid-map from the travel guide, mispronouncing all the street names so badly that we gave up trying to talk about it. Out of hunger we settled for Subway, the only American chain restaurant in sight, but one that was guaranteed to have vegetarian food. It's actually Danielle's favorite restaurant. We heard hardcore music coming from a bar around the corner, so we walked over to check it out.

Day Two: Reykjavik in December gets about four hours of sunlight. In the morning I walked to a bus terminal so I could e-mail Bragi and Michael and alert them to our presence in Reykjavik. The four of us met at Nelly's, the bar Danielle and I had discovered last night and which turned out to be the only cheap place in town to drink. We found out the hardcore band was on Bragi's record label, Bad Taste, and we followed him down the street so he could give us a CD from his house. Inside we kept him up 'til 5 AM listening to CDs and talking about music and books, me asking for stories about his old band the Sugarcubes. He made coffee for us and opened two small containers of milk. I gave him the box of Alka-Seltzer he'd asked me to smuggle into Iceland. For some reason it's outlawed here. "I had to stick that up my ass," I told him. We drank more coffee and listened to more music. All night he kept giving us stuff. If we liked a CD that was playing, he'd run into the other room and dig through boxes to find one for us. He gave us a copy of his first book of poetry and an anthology from Ordid Tonlist, a word and music festival he and Michael put together last year. He had to work at the ad agency at 9 o'clock, but when Danielle and I left just past five, he said he was going to stay up and read for awhile. He kissed Danielle on both cheeks and we left with our arms full of CDs and books.

Day Three: We met up with Michael at Nelly's. Three days in town and we already had settled into a routine. Michael took us to Graen Kostur, a vegetarian restaurant two blocks away. The place was so good I made him retrace the route for us. I wanted to eat there the next day. Every day we went to Graen Kostur; every night we went to Nelly's. In between we saw the Blue Lagoon, waited outside in 10-degree weather for them to open the doors to the geothermal steam lake. I took amazing pictures of Danielle on the rocky shore with black mountains behind her. We kept Michael company while he worked at his bookstore. I dropped my books there and at Mal og Menning down the street, where Danielle and I sat upstairs drinking hot chocolate, dipping pieces of chocolate bars into it. We went up the tower at Hallgrimskirkja, a church with a view of the entire city. Michael told us they put bars on the windows of the tower because people kept leaping out of it during these months when the sun never shines — bodies slamming against the slope of the church on their way to the ground.

Day Four: Our last morning in town we saw the Iceland Phallogical Museum, the only museum in the world devoted to the penis. It's open only two days a week, from 10 AM to 2 PM, and we had to catch a bus to the airport at 11 AM, so we were waiting outside when they opened the doors. Danielle was skeptical that we could make it in time, but I was determined to see the dick museum before we left Reykjavik. Inside we were surrounded by specimens from every species of animal that inhabits Iceland, and contracts on the wall from humans willing their cocks to the museum upon their deaths. We viewed it all in fast-forward, circling the two small rooms at a steady pace. No time to stop and study any of it, just get a sense of it, an impression, and move on. Our run back to Hotel Loftleider was the same, a speed-through flipbook of all the sites we'd remember from Reykjavik: Hallgrimskirkja, the graveyard, Michael's bookstore with the Santa Clauses creeping up the side of the building like cat burglars, the shop where we bought pastries and chocolate bars, Ingollstraeti — the street where we always turned the wrong way and got lost, Leif Eriksson statue, the observatory, and back to collect our luggage and get on the bus.

That's how I would experience things for the next few months, glancing sideways getting a quick impression, but no time to stop and really consider what I saw. Teaching, the ice cream truck, Digital Underground — it all flew past me peripherally. And now my plans are confirmed to bring Bragi and Michael to read and speak at Indiana University Southwest, which means forms to fill out, reservations for flights and hotels, and weird budgetary concerns that require math skills I have long forgotten.

Michael Pollock is hyper with sleepy eyes. He smiles a lot, which is either because of happiness or because his hearing is not good and it's easier to smile than ask people to say things louder. "Too much punk rock!" He has perfect teeth.

Bragi smells like coffee, cigarettes, and the licorice gummies he brought us from Iceland. He was searched at the airport while Michael made it through metal detectors with the homemade black-jack his brother gave him before he left — "You watch out for those American gangs."

I meet them at the airport at midnight Louisville time, but it's 5 AM in Iceland and they look tired. Michael tells us how he was wedged in between two huge bikers on the connecting flight from Baltimore. "They wouldn't talk!" They spoke two sentences across him before they took off, and that was it:

There's a lot of people on here.
Yep.

It worked! All the forms I filled out have found their way to the right offices and everything is approved. My three-week selection process for the perfect travel agent has paid off. I put together this event in such a hurry that most expenses are charged to my credit card up front and I trust the university to reimburse me. I'm used to doing everything for myself and trying to keep expenses at a minimum, so I was responsible for every aspect of the event, from securing funding to stapling the fliers. "Word and Culture: Iceland to Indiana" — address all questions to Mickey Hess, Project Director.

I've stopped more than once to consider why I wanted to take on all the extra work of bringing Bragi and Michael to campus. Michael had mentioned the idea our last night in Reykjavik, but it was a pass-ing suggestion. I'm sure he never really expected me to contact him three months later and say "Ready to go?" Was this for some kind of personal gain? Taking advantage of the possibilities of my new official job status? Last night I received an email from the Dean, congratulat-ing me on making it happen — "You really desire a lot of credit for this." The typo made me think. Was that really the reason I've done all this? To see if I *could* do it? Am I looking for credit?

Bragi is fascinated with Decimus. It's illegal to own iguanas in Iceland, where they might escape and wreck the ecosystem before freezing to death. He kneels down and runs his finger along her tail. "She's beautiful," he says. "She looks like a dragon." I show him how to mimic iguana body language so that she won't think he's aggressive. I show him the leash and harness we bought to take her for walks. There are too many dogs at public parks, but the campus is a perfect spot. Decimus loves to climb trees, and that's hard to replicate inside, so I pick a small one and let her climb as high as the leash will extend. She sits there on a branch of the tree, and I stand there holding the leash. One day the chair of the English department walked by and we exchanged greetings. From the look on his face you'd think the guy had never seen anyone walking an iguana before. It looked like it both scared and annoyed him. It wasn't until he walked away that I realized he couldn't even see Decimus there on her branch, so it looked like I was standing in the middle of campus with a string tied to a tree. This is the impression I make on my colleagues.

Danielle and I rescued Decimus from a philosophy professor whose wife had thought an iguana would make a great pet for her second-grade classroom. After twenty-five second graders had thoroughly traumatized Decimus, she brought her home to stay in a basement with two large dogs. This is when Decimus learned to break out of her aquarium — that small panel of glass didn't seem like enough protection from predators. She slept at the top of the curtains, where no dogs or second-graders could reach her, and she learned to use her tail as a weapon. She didn't even have a name. They just called her "the lizard." One day Dr. Padgett walked into the philosophy office and asked, "Do any of ya'll want a big green lizard?" Danielle jumped at the opportunity.

We named Decimus after a cartoon character from our *Introduction to Latin* textbook. In the Latin book, Decimus was a kid who brought a knife to school and attacked the professor. It seemed to fit with the iguana's initial reaction to Danielle and me. You can't blame her. She had a rough childhood. She was terrified of us when we brought her home, but now she loves nothing more than to eat prunes and bananas out of our hands. I ask Bragi if he wants to feed her a banana, and he falls as much in love with her as Danielle and I have. Decimus will become the basis for a central character in Bragi's next novel. He has a commission from the Icelandic government to write a novel and two plays in the next two years. I don't ask him how much the grant pays, but it's enough for him to quit his job at the ad agency and write full time. Bragi's wishing he lived in the U.S., where he can get iguanas and Alka-Seltzer, and I'm wishing I lived in Iceland, where the government pays people to write books.

Michael hands me the Icelandic newspaper. He hasn't had a chance to sit down and translate it for me, but there it is, on the front page of the culture section, a picture of *El Cumpleanos de Paco*.

"Punnur Pretandi? What's that mean?"

"Um, it doesn't really translate directly." Michael looks at Bragi, who nods. "It basically means *nothing much*."

"Nothing much? The title of the book review is *Nothing Much*?"

❋ ❋ ❋

There's a tractor convention in Louisville this weekend, so all the central and remotely affordable hotels are booked in the region that is unfortunately known as Kentuckiana, which includes Louisville and its suburbs, as well as the Indiana towns on the other side of the river. Finally we settle for one room with two beds at a Suburban Lodge near the Louisville city limits and near absolutely nothing else. Michael and Bragi woke up their first morning in Louisville, walked two miles down the side of the highway, and the only food in sight was Burger King. Bragi told me about his Croissan'wich later that afternoon. "It was shaped like a croissant," he said. "But it was not a croissant."

We wake up early for a public radio interview and then we listen to Lightnin' Hopkins' "Early Mornin Blues" on our drive up to IU Southwest, where Bragi and Michael will speak to my classes this morning. They drink whiskey in the gravel parking lot before my 9:30 class. I won't let them sneak in a hip flask. Our campus has cracked down on alcohol regulations. Zero Tolerance. Campus security takes it seriously. Someone told me that the semester before I started working here, they busted up an English department party and confiscated their wine.

Bragi in Norse mythology is the god of poetry. We think about introducing him that way at our reading: up next, the Norse God of Poetry. Bragi's voice over a saxophone track has a nice David Lynch quality to it. We do a very half-ass sound check with Dave, the pony-tailed IUS sound technician, who gives us a thumbs-up from the booth. He's ready. The music levels are good but let's check the acoustics. Bragi reads "How to Behave Among the Locals":

I hear myself whisper beautiful things into strangers´ ears.
I shall stand as if in uniform
on my own two feet.
I shall topple over
and think while falling:
I am the darling of fortune

60

Michael reads from "Paradise Lost":

... I slept for days on end and ate meagerly. Eventually I pulled my ass out of the bed, put my shoes on, went out and got a job. Janitor at a mall. I worked third shift. Twilight Zone. The graveyard shift. Sometimes I would go down to the mall on days off. That's where I met Janet. By the fountain. She was throwin' coins into the water, makin' wishes. Little did she know in the middle of the night I plucked her wishes out of the water and pumped them into vending machines ...

Dave assures us the echo will go away. In a few hours the Robinson Theater will not be this empty. There will be fifty bodies to absorb these sounds and messages. I will give them each a dull pencil and a survey form — "Word and Culture was entertaining," "Word and Culture promoted international understanding and a valuable exchange of culture" — each of them can agree, or strongly disagree. Each can be "not sure." They will fill in small bubbles to match their choices. This will please the Humanities Council.

I will ask Bragi and Michael questions to which I already know the answers. I will remark that Led Zeppelin called Iceland the land of ice and snow. "Is this accurate?" I will ask. I will ask them about the penis museum. They will read poetry. People will clap. Eyes will water.

※ ※ ※

The Shithouse Poets are playing a show tonight and I'm bringing Michael and Bragi. Activated Peat is opening the show. Their fliers say "Activated Peat Presents ..." and every show they change the name of the band they're presenting. Their first show it was the Virgins. Tonight, Captain Clapp and the STDs. They dress in second-hand military uniforms and giant bushy wigs. The singer has a stuffed cat sticking through the zipper of his pants. They make up new names for themselves. "On drums we have Colonel Clamydia, on bass, General Warts." The singer is Captain Clapp. The guitarist is Sergeant Syphillis.

The STDs are just wrapping up as we enter the Hideaway Saloon. Michael gets stopped at the door — his ID proves he's 44 years old but he's met with a bouncer who seems suspicious that Iceland is a real place. We find a table and I introduce Michael and Bragi to people while one band tears down and the other sets up, all in a matter of minutes — they share a drum kit, and a drummer. Icehouse beers are a dollar tonight and the show itself is free. Shithouse Poets shows are always free or at least dirt cheap. "Drink up, everybody," they tell us when they hit the stage. "We get a cut of the alcohol sales."

I met the Shithouse Poets through Danielle's friend Tracy. Shithouse Brad came to Michael and Bragi's reading and invited us to see his show. Brad and I share an interest in homemade t-shirts, but tonight he's wearing a great find from his day job at Goodwill, a shirt that says "Make it legal: do it with a lawyer." The shirt is old and black and too tight and the white vinyl letters are chipping off.

The Poets open with "Woke up Hungry," a song about zombies that they always dedicate to Tracy, who searches out horror movies at flea markets. She's genuinely excited to see us tonight. Tracy gets more genuinely excited about things than anyone else. Sometimes Danielle and I give her random presents just because her reaction is always so perfect.

> Last night when I woke up, my eyes were sewn shut
> Had an achin' pain in my head, and a hunger in my gut

Michael gets a kick out of Aidan, a 65-year old scenester and friend of Tracy and Brad. The whole show he stands right in front yelling *Do it you motherfuckers! Don't stop now I'm about to explode!* The whole place sounds crunchy. The stage is so tiny that the band plays in front of it. All that's on stage are the drums and an amp that says "Crud Rock" across the front.

I've seen the Shithouse Poets play before, but watching them through the eyes of Michael and Bragi makes me appreciate them even more. There's so much Louisville I want to show Michael and Bragi that it can't fit into one week. But tomorrow we're going to the Colonel Sanders museum, and we're drinking with the Shithouse Poets tonight.

❖ ❖ ❖

Maybe math works different in Iceland, but when Bragi finally hands me the English version of my book review, it's nowhere near forty percent positive. It's closer to four percent positive. I guess that's why he waited until I drove him back to the airport to hand it to me. "That's just a rough translation," he said.

As you can imagine, a book review titled "Nothing Much" is full of such praise as "We hear about some boring characters," and "Perhaps it is unfair to expect a writer to have something to say."

The review is crushing. I will stay depressed about it for weeks, and write the reviewer an angry letter I never send, and stare at my writing and feel beaten down and discouraged by the whole experience until some Icelanders and Swedes start to write me asking for copies of the book. Finally I throw the translation away and hang the newspaper clipping on the wall over my desk. I can feel good that at least I got reviewed. Nobody in Kentucky speaks Icelandic anyway. Sometimes it works for me — I only remember two or three phrases from Bragi's translation — but sometimes I look at that newspaper clipping and feel like everything I work so hard on will end up being nothing much.

Summer Break

Seven

I applied for a job at Action World Family Fun Center after I won six straight games of air hockey against Jake, Carrie, and Danielle. I was the fucking air hockey champion. I have this move, a quick forehand flick-of-the-wrist bank shot, that can be just unstoppable when I get into my pattern, and I was into it that day. I don't know what it is about arcade sports games. I am completely untalented when it comes to sports and not that good at video games, but when it comes to the combination — air hockey, Basketball Supershoot — they're all mine.

Action World is a giant indoor amusement park that takes up the entire second floor of a mall in southern Indiana. You can play miniature golf there. You can ride a train around the perimeter of the food court. Jake convinced me to ask for an application and let me borrow his pen to fill it out. It was three weeks into the summer and everything seemed to stretch out in front of me — all my plans for new things to write, to do, all this time away from my teaching schedule — and since when did Jake start carrying a pen around with him? It struck me as an unexpected addition to his personality.

Called back for an interview I feel the crunch, that rush of urgency and dread that I feel whenever I get a job, because it's going to change everything, my existence as it has been the past few weeks. When you're a kid they pull you out of the house one day and put you in school and for a long time you don't even question it. It seems like some kind of adventure the first few years, but then summers start to mean so much and it gets harder and harder to go back in the fall. That's how I feel today, like when I was a kid and no matter how long the summer was dragging on or how bored I was sitting inside all day watching *Divorce Court* and *The Price is Right*, I still didn't want to go back to school. No matter how boring leisure gets, it's comfortable, and it's addictive.

It's summer, and there's no reason for me to work, but I am teaching one class for some extra money. Summer is also the perfect time to take an iguana for walks on campus. Not only are there no dogs, but there are very few people as well. While Danielle's on her shift at the zoo, I drive to campus with Decimus in a cardboard Amazon.com box in the back seat. I have the flaps folded into each other but she still escapes and climbs onto the headrest behind me, then across my face and onto the steering wheel.

I park, stuff Decimus back into the box, and walk past the humanities building just in time to run into the chair of the English department, the same man who saw me standing in the middle of campus with a string tied to a tree. We say hello and agree that we don't like plagiarism, and that summer courses are generally more casual than fall or spring. He's beginning to think I might be normal after all. Here I am on my day off, on campus with what appears to be a box full of books. Then, while I'm debating whether to tell him that I came here to walk my iguana, Decimus bursts out of the box.

❊ ❊ ❊

I was complaining earlier about those college professors who take paid time off from their teaching gigs to work a series of blue collar jobs. John Coleman did it in the sixties, and Barbara Ehrenreich in the nineties. They disguised themselves as non-academics and got jobs at farms and restaurants and shopping centers. What I don't understand is the deceit — they both pretended to be people they weren't so they could get close to their interview subjects, and then at the end they revealed, "Oh, and by the way, I'm a professor. All of our conversations have really been interviews for a book I'm writing. Don't worry, I'll change your name." It isn't only an ethical question. It's one of necessity. Maybe when Coleman did it in the sixties, being a college professor meant something different and he did need to pretend to be someone he wasn't. But today I don't think the job holds that much prestige. And to prove it, I'm going to be absolutely forthcoming in my Action World interview.

Action World becomes less festive as I'm led into its inner workings, long concrete hallways lined with broken-down pinball machines lead to the main office, in the bowels of the mall. The manager, Barbara, is a sour, overbearing woman who is negotiating a schedule change as I wait outside her office. Two employees want to switch shifts on Thursday, and she rules that they can do it as long as they have no delusions about who holds the scheduling power: "As long as you understand that I'm doing you a favor, and that you'll work whenever *I say* you'll work, not when you say you will." This is the first words I hear Barbara speak, and I won't forget them.

My interview sticks to the basics at first. Most of Barbara's questions come directly from a typed sheet: "What do you think you can add to the Action World team? What would you say is your single greatest accomplishment?" She then leads me through safety precautions and tries to scare me into submission by relating two stories of near-disasters, recent employee fuck-ups. Kids nearly crippled by bumper cars, dangling from Pilot Patrol in mid-flight. She reiterates the sign on her desk — "*No* cell phones while you're working. People get wrapped up in their conversations and aren't watching the kids."

She points to the employment history section of my application — "College instructor, huh? My daughter wants to be a teacher. She would've been in college by now but she got pregnant." She frowns, shakes her head. "What kind of classes do you teach?"

"Writing mainly … 20th Century American Lit … next fall I get to teach a 400-level Fiction workshop."

"So, you more interested in working like the bumper cars or the merry-go-round?"

We move on to rules of conduct for Action World employees. I have to buy my own uniform, and I can never play games while wearing it, whether on or off the clock. Breaks are to be taken in the breakroom, a dingy gray box separated from the mechanical repair shop by a chain-link gate. Barbara leads me through the breakroom, pointing out the water fountain and folding table. "You can buy your food in the food court," she says, "But you have to eat it in here."

❊ ❊ ❊

My first night at Action World I was trained and had to take a short certification quiz. As of today I am certified to teach college, operate an ice cream truck, and maintain a pit filled with plastic multicolored balls. I was stationed at Megazone, right around the corner from Toddler Town.

Working the ball pit was easy. Going in to fill out paperwork was the hard part, and so was acclimating myself. It took me almost an hour to adjust to my new environment, and to having an immediate supervisor. When I'm teaching, no one's really looking over my shoulder, keeping track of how I spend my time. But here I feel like the kids who are

69

being watched by their parents as they play in Megazone. "Don't run!" "Don't put your mouth on that thing!" "Don't hit that little girl." I was afraid to leave my post to go to the restroom. After that first hour though, I loosened up and didn't worry about my bosses. After all, the only thing more fun than working the ball pit would be getting fired from it.

The inevitable happened tonight and I ran into one of my students, Jonathan, who works at a store called Structure For Men on the first floor of the mall. We saw each other from opposite ends of the food court, and he made the connection immediately. There's no mistaking the $12 black polo shirt with gold armband — the Action World uniform I had to buy myself. "Do you *work* here?"

Working Megazone is fun enough. I was trained by a high school senior named Monica, who spent most of the night talking me through a picture album from her recent trip to San Francisco. When I was staring clueless at the Megazone certification quiz, Monica leaned over the padded railing and whispered all the answers. She got most of them wrong, but I guess the managers have pretty low expectations.

Anytime Megazone was empty of kids, we took off our shoes and looked for change in the ball pit. From what Monica told me, the creases between the foam blocks on the bottom are like goldmines. She and her boyfriend found 28 dollars in change one Saturday night, digging around and feeling for coins with their toes. Tonight is a Thursday, though, just before the weekend stampede of kids, so Monica's take was limited to 58 cents. I found two dimes and a Spiderman band-aid.

Loose change isn't the only thing kids leave behind in the plastic balls. As the certification test puts it:

True or False: When the Megazone attendant discovers any "messes," he or she should clear the area and disinfect Megazone before children can re-enter.

Kids jump in and piss and shit and vomit and stick their gum and band-aids all over the place, and it's our job to look out for it and clean it up. A little girl lost her mom's wedding ring in the pit tonight and Monica and I had to go pit-digging all over again. The ring never turned up.

There's something to be said for a job that lets you work in your socks. I spent most of the night sitting on a padded ramp with my back against Megazone, oblivious this way to any hair-pulling, barefoot kids climbing up the slide instead of down, breaking three rules at once. An electronic bowling machine was jammed and malfunctioning, and serenaded me all night with "Please take ticket please take ticket please take ticket. . .." in this high-pitched cartoon mouse voice. It was annoying for the first two hours, but started to maintain such a rhythm that I spent 8-9 o'clock half asleep. There was nothing to do. Megazone is for young kids, 45 inches and under, and by an hour to closing they've either lost interest or been taken home by their parents.

Monica has been married since March 25. Two months, and she's been pregnant for three. She tells me she had to undergo outpatient surgery to remove a cyst from the baby's head. "The doctor said it could come out retarded if we didn't take care of it now. I'm still sore." She shows me her engagement ring, with a real ruby and two small, real diamonds. "My wedding ring is at the jewelry repair downstairs. It had real diamonds too, but they fell out." Danielle and I bought our wedding rings in a pawnshop. I bought her engagement ring from a 25-cent machine in front of Wal-Mart.

❈ ❈ ❈

I am expected to dress more formally to operate the Big Rigs ride at Action World than I do to teach. I spent $12 on the required black polo shirt with the gold armband, and tucked it neatly into my khaki pants. I spent the first two hours of work earning back the money I paid for the shirt. I complained to Monica about it the first night, but she said it was nothing compared to the uniforms at her high school.

I'm thankful I missed the school uniform movement in public high schools, although I never really had any sense of personal style until senior year, when my art teacher Mr. Dixon showed me how to silkscreen t-shirts by hand. Silk-screening was one of the first projects we did, but it was all my friends and I worked on for the rest of the year. Mark and James and I almost failed the class because we refused to move on to sculpture or watercolors. We just sat in the back of the art room every day and made t-shirts. It was frustrating for Mr. Dixon, but I don't think he had any idea what a huge influence he had on us. A few weeks ago, Mark's band Hell Nation played at a club here in Louisville, and I met up with him and James before the show. I was wearing the new shirt I had just finished the night before, and they were both taking the day off from their jobs at competing silk-screen companies back in Somerset, Kentucky. They sneak in late at night to make shirts and patches with their band logos.

Lately I've been designing shirts with violent cartoons on them. The most recent one is a bizarre illustration from Danielle's old Spanish textbook — a used car dealer smacking another guy in the face — *¡Que ∂ia terible!* When I teach, I wear my homemade t-shirts and the same jeans I'd wear anywhere. I'm glad the dress code for university employees is nothing specific like Action World, just something implied or assumed. When I go in to turn in my grades at the Registrar's office, I watch them eye me with sincere mistrust — they notice but don't acknowledge me, keep me standing at the counter a few minutes before asking "Can I help you?" in a voice that makes it clear that I obviously am a person who needs help, needs it to the extent that I am in all likelihood in the absolute wrong place for the kind of help that I need. That's what they're just waiting to do at a university, you realize. Send you on to the next office.

❊ ❊ ❊

As of today, I am certified to press the green button to start the Big Rig convoy moving. The Big Rigs are one of the most boring rides to be assigned to, from what everyone tells me. Miniature semi-truck cabs with room inside for two very small children and a platform in the back for the ones who can't fit inside. Most often the back seat is used by adults who come in with small children who sit up front. From across the food court, it looks like grown men are perched on the Big Rigs all by themselves, riding in slow, steady circles around the track.

The best thing to see is when real-life truckers, home for the weekend, bring their children to ride the Big Rigs. One guy who was too overweight to fit into the back seat let his young son —barely old enough to stand up on his own — ride by himself while he cheered from the parents' area, banging on the railing and yelling to the other parents, "Whew! He's really gettin off on this!"

I spent six hours standing in front of a train of small semi-trucks, helping kids open the doors and fasten their seatbelts, and sounding the horn here and there during the ride to make it seem more authentic. Someone has etched "Fuck You" into the back of the operator's station, and "This Sucks As" into the Big Rigs Rules for Safety.

❊ ❊ ❊

I ended my class five minutes early and changed into my Action

World work clothes in a downstairs IUS bathroom stall. Like Clark Kent to Superman. I grabbed my black polo shirt and khaki pants out of the lecturers' office and ran downstairs undetected. I felt secretive again because I had run into two full-time professors from the English department earlier in the writing lab and I didn't want them to see I'd switched clothes and then question why I was dressed more professionally on my way *out* of work. As stealthy as I tried to be, there they were sitting outside the front door when I left the building.

It's thunder-storming outside and the mall is dead. I can see lightning outside the white plexiglass dome that covers the elevator shaft. The arcade is empty but the machines go on beeping and blinking and flashing. I'm sitting on one of the foam floor pads in front of Megazone, with my back against the entrance to the ball pit, writing in this tiny spiral notebook Danielle bought me for Valentine's Day four years ago. There's only one little girl in Megazone, and she's been in here for almost an hour and a half now, running in circles non-stop. Her dad is asleep on a bench.

Half the rides sit motionless because we're short-handed tonight. Two people called in sick or without transportation, and one person called in to quit. I started tonight on the Thrillrider, a van-shaped gray box that mimics the motion of a space shuttle while kids watch asteroids and alien warships fly at them on the video screen inside. What I do is open and close the doors and read a short safety message before I press the sequence of buttons that starts the ride.

The best thing about working the Thrillrider is that the operator's station is equipped with a tiny speaker that lets me monitor the inside in case any kids get scared and want to get out. Of course nobody realizes I can listen to them, and so can anybody standing within ten feet of me. My favorite is the junior high kids. They know all the words for cursing, but don't really have a good sense of how to use them together. I'll hear random phrases come out, like "Dick-Ass!" "Pussy whore!" Their moms in the parent area stand aghast.

✤ ✤ ✤

I skipped my next shift at Action World. I don't know what it was, but I just couldn't bring myself to go in. It was a beautiful day outside, the first truly sunny day we'd had in two weeks. I was scheduled to work from noon to six, but I went and ate Mexican food with Jake and Danielle and Carrie. We played basketball and threw water balloons at each other. I don't know if it was the fact that I had twenty papers from my class to read over the weekend, or if I'm just getting used to my simulated lazy rich kid existence, but I knew even the night before that I wouldn't go.

I planned to call in at first, either to make an excuse for the one day or to quit for good, depending on how they received my excuse. But as I was putting off the phone call, I thought back to that first day at my interview, two kids asking to switch schedules and Barbara the manager saying, "They'll work when *I* say they'll work!" I hate it when bosses say things like that, take any opportunity to remind you they're in charge. What gets me about Barbara is that she was doing what the employees wanted, letting them switch schedules, but she wouldn't let the favor slip by without a speech. So wouldn't it be great if I *didn't* call, but still showed up at my scheduled time the following day, acting like nothing happened?

"So what happened yesterday?"

"I don't know. I wasn't here." Completely straightforward and calm. Show them that I'll work when *I* say I will.

So I skipped that day, and I go in this afternoon late. It seems like such a good added effect that I walk around the sporting goods store downstairs for 15 minutes before I take the escalator to Action World. Barbara has gone home by this time, leaving Amanda the assistant manager in charge for the night. I get some puzzled stares from fellow Action World workers on my way in through the arcade to the administrative offices in the back, where it is as if I have never existed. I've been erased from the running timelog and the day's schedule on the huge dry-erase board.

Barbara made her executive decision, but I guess she forgot to pass the word. On my way out of the breakroom, Amanda catches me and assigns me again to the Big Rigs. Not even a word about my disappearing act yesterday. I am still not officially certified to operate the Big Rigs, and when I mention this, Amanda hands me a packet of exams:

Write the instructional speech for the Big Rigs:

Keep your head and arms inside the Big Rigs at all times. No whistling old trucker tunes.

Can you talk to your friends on your cell phone while operating the ride? Explain in detail why <u>not</u>.

The Big Rigs can interfere with your reception and you end up having to shout so your friends can understand you. One time I was talking to my friend Jake about chewing gum or something like that and he said he's allergic to fake cinnamon. But I thought he said cinema — "I'm allergic to fake cinema." I was like OK, Jake. Whatever.

I complete three tests — Pilot Patrol, Thrillrider, and the Big Rigs — sometimes answering in cartoon illustration form. I turn on the Big Rig headlights, check the track for debris, and sit down, stuck. I look around at Monica filing her fingernails by the prize booth, Brian asleep in Megazone. How many of us need to be here anyway? If we stayed home, would the merry-go-round keep on spinning? Would the bumper cars monitor themselves?

I can't handle it. Nothing against the Big Rigs, but I came in expecting to be fired and sent home. I'm not in the mindset to stand here all night sounding the realistic trucker horn. At the first opportunity, my first break from kids in line, I shut the control panel and run. Past the breakroom, out through the door by the main office. Amanda's sitting at a table in front of the food court, right beside the stairs to the exit. I rush past her and she gives me this confused, speechless look.

People ask me if I still work at Action World and I tell them I don't know. No one's ever called to say I was fired. I've never called to say I quit. This could go on all summer. Danielle's idea is that I go in at random, weeks from now — just show up in my black polo shirt ready to operate some rides.

Eight

If you ever need someone to house sit, don't ask Danielle and me. The last time we house sat for Dr. Rebecca Pederson, it ended with one dead finch, a thoroughly crashed computer, and a broken garage door opener. And now she's calling us again.

None of these were our fault, specifically, but still I feel awful about them. The bird was sick when we got there, but we watched it steadily decline and watched its companion turn on it when it became weak enough. That's what killed it, the bird that had been sitting beside it in a cage for ten years, just waiting for the opportunity. I had to scoop its body into an empty pizza box and weigh down the lid of the garbage can to keep the cats and dogs out. The computer and the garage door I can't explain. If I could blame that evil bird, though, I would.

I didn't break that garage door opener or crash that computer, but it happened on my watch, so I took full responsibility. I left Rebecca an apology note when she got back home. If I were her, though, I would not want me back in my house.

Danielle and I move into the house again yesterday. We're left with keys, an envelope full of cash, and three fully stocked refrigerators that we're encouraged to treat as our own. Dr. Rebecca's house is filled with free clocks and hand lotions and notepads and chip clips, all from drug companies. There are Clarinex potholders, a Ditropan umbrella. Rebecca is a general practitioner with a side interest in holistic medicine. She's a Buddhist and plays stand-up bass in a bluegrass band. She likes poetry too. Danielle and I were introduced to her when she came to see Michael and Bragi's reading — it was the first time we met her, and the first time she asked us to house sit.

Our primary responsibilities as house sitters are to throw frisbees to the dogs and make sure the biggest one doesn't eat the food meant for the other two. Shiva, the German Shepherd, just lives for frisbee. The first night we spend at the house, she's been locked in her backyard kennel for probably nine or ten hours, and the first thing she goes for is the frisbee. She chases it relentlessly, so much that she gets the other dogs, Sniper and Savannah, worked up and they start cheering her on. Sniper's so old that the only way he can play is to bark in encouragement. His eyes are glazed over with cataracts so he's not even sure what it is that's so exciting. He just senses some energy.

Danielle is excited to live with three dogs for a few weeks. Between our pets at home, her job at the zoo, and this housesitting gig, she's spending all her time around animals this summer. Staying at Rebecca's feels like I'm living the rich-kid suburban lifestyle I missed out on when I lived with my parents. The house is twenty minutes outside of Louisville, in Floyds Knobs, Indiana. The back yard faces the woods. Rebecca has a basketball hoop in front of her garage and a deck with a hot tub out back. This is the kind of house I remember visiting as a kid, the houses of high school friends that I always envied. It seems like the perfect place to skip school when your parents aren't home. Maybe that's why house sitting has contributed to my laziness. Danielle's too. We play with the dogs all day and lounge around in the hot tub all night. Invite Jake and Carrie over to watch cable, which is a surprising luxury when you don't have it at your own house. This is our summer vacation.

These first days of June have been dark and cloudy, though. It rains briefly and sporadically throughout the day and night, but more often it's just on the verge of raining. This weather is affecting us. We spend most of the day questioning what we're going to do next, when we haven't even finished what we're doing now. We don't get into the hot tub spontaneously, but discuss if we should get in now, or maybe watch TV for an hour and then get in. I feel anxious, like something's about to happen.

House sitting has made us sluggish. When we go home to our own apartment, it feels like we've been out somewhere, when all we've been doing is sitting around someone else's house. We've been trying to divide our time equally so that we don't neglect our own pets or the ones we're being paid to watch. Most of our plans outside the house involve driving between these places. I taught my classes on Monday and Wednesday, and I played tennis with Jake one night while Danielle watched *Buffy the Vampire Slayer* with Carrie, but basically this week has been void of any social activity.

✧✧✧

This morning I present at a faculty colloquium my latest project, "Wasting Our Educated Minds: Student Resistance in College Movies." I have handouts. I use a projector. I discuss college movies as a subgenre of teen films, as a last stand against life as career. I talk about the career student, the guy in all these movies who has been in school for seven years and never intends to leave. "Why are these characters always men?" I question. I trace the phenomena back to *Animal House*, to Bluto, a career student who earns a 0.0 GPA in his seventh year as an undergraduate, and is more interested in Jack Daniels and toga parties than attending class. I call this "prolonged postponement." I quote Stanley Aronowitz.

I make points about higher education as training, about political generations and alternative forms of resistance. In the 1960s, American students worked together to change the system through collective action, and the university was a site of resistance. In the 1990s, most student resistance occurred at the level of the individual. Students rejected collective action for the most part, and when they did organize, it was often against the university itself.

"Ultimately," I say, "The career student is a figure of satire, but also may serve to offer sagelike advice to a younger character. The career student presents himself to freshmen as someone who has spent so long at college that he's figured out how to manipulate, exploit, or sabotage the culture of higher education." I stop there. My colleagues cock their heads. They put pens to their lips and then nod as if they've learned something important.

✧✧✧

Over the past three years, we've started a tradition of celebrating Halloween twice a year, with a second one in early June. Jake hates it even in October. He is easily frightened, and is particularly unexcited about this year's Halloween-in-June because this is the last day of his two-week vacation from work. I recycle Danielle's evil clown costume from last year and top it off with Carrie's neon blue wig and some of her red shimmer lipstick. Carrie's an undead bride in a thrift-store wedding gown and a jet back pigtailed wig. All the time Carrie and I are preparing in the mirror upstairs and Jake is sulking watching the Food Network downstairs, we have no idea where Danielle is. But I know she's working on something good. She emerges from the basement in a tight black nylon facemask she made from pantyhose, a black skirt and tank top and a pair of human-sized insect wings. She looks like a dark, vindictive fairy.

We've been preparing for this night for two weeks. The original June Halloween happened on the spur of the moment, but three years later we make mix tapes of spooky or otherwise fitting music, we stockpile makeup in the days after October 31 — it's half-price then and it's tough to find it in June, we scour Salvation Army stores for clothes we can turn into costumes. On the actual night, we might switch costumes four times, or trade with each other — it's all part of the fun. Inevitably, before the night is over, I end up in a dress.

Jake won't put on a costume, but he does take pictures. We have it all documented — the forest marriage of Clown Boy and Evil June Dead, Danielle's black fairy rituals ... we blast our scary mix tapes from the speakers until Jake gets tired of it and I switch back to Ghostface Killah. While we're outside, the lights come on in a room upstairs and Jake is convinced there's somebody in the house. He makes me crack open the door to Rebecca's bedroom, the one forbidden room in the house, because that's where the light was coming from. "She's a fucking witch, man. She never even left home, she's just been up in her bedroom watching us this whole time." Even after I show him the security lights in Rebecca's bedroom that are probably set to a timer, he's truly scared, so much that he asks Carrie if she's ready to leave.

After they go, Danielle and I make fun of Jake. But the house is quieter now that it's emptier, and some of his fear gets transferred to me. The paintings in the basement look menacing, and when I walk down the stairs their faces see me coming.

**

It isn't technically a party. Rebecca's house sitting rules say no parties, but she couldn't count this one against us. I mean, we're allowed to invite two friends at a time — one other couple, she said — and all we've done is doubled that. Only six of us, here to celebrate Will's new job at the American Printing House for the Blind. He's followed in Danielle's footsteps and gotten a job off campus. That's two of us now. The rest of us remain the perfect employees. We pay for an education, and fearing it has prepared us for nothing else, we come back.

Our night begins innocently enough. Jake takes stock of the refrigerators, but we aren't greedy. We use only one box of veggie burgers, even supply our own buns. Rebecca has three refrigerators. She keeps one in her garage full of cheese pizzas and Garden burgers and whole bean coffee for when the coffee inside runs out. This supplements the basement refrigerator — which is all ginger ale, root beer, dog medicine, and regular beer (Old Milwaukee) — and the main refrigerator in the kitchen, which seems to be mostly condiments and a small ration of soft drinks for those moments when the stairs down to the basement seem like too much effort to make. So we eat modestly, and we buy our own alcohol. I play Nice & Smooth because Will and Lara have never heard of them.

"Greg Nice and Smooth B?"
"No, it doesn't ring a bell."
"Hip Hop Junkies? Funky 4 You?"
"No."

Will recognizes a sample from *The Partridge Family*. Lara tells us that as a kid the only music she ever listened to was Weird Al Yankovic — "And I'm not sure I even got that they were parodies, considering I'd never heard the originals. I went to my friend's birthday party one year and they were all singing Like a Virgin. Well, I was singing Like a Surgeon."

It really isn't a party — at least not a good one. Not at this point. Jake and Lara share complaints from the advising office, where no students come to see them for four months straight, and then everyone shows up the last two days you can register:

Lara: Can't stand to rush a student through the process when there are so many other students waiting to be advised.

Jake: Tired of Lara taking 45 minutes talking to one student while all her extras pile up in his line.

Lara: Hates when students think her name is LAURa— "I learned your name. Least you can do is get mine right."

Jake: Wishes students wouldn't wear low-rise jeans — "you can see girls' *underwear*" — or halter tops when they come to his office.

Lara: "What are you talking about?"

Danielle: "Ok, Grandpa."

Lara, Danielle, and Carrie debate Jake until he admits he doesn't like these clothes because he finds them distracting, and when he's distracted *who knows* what courses he's signing these women into? They come in needing a science credit and walk out enrolled in Beginning Fencing. Danielle later helps me create a sign for Jake's office door:

What Should I Wear to my Advising Appointment?

Think Sunday School.
Ask yourself, WWJRW — What Would Jake Roebuck Wear?
NO thongs*
Look to classic television for models of appropriate dress:
Charlie's Angels — Not Appropriate, Little House on the Prairie — Appropriate, Aunt Bea — Preferred.

Will drinks Malibu. On a night like this, he will buy a new bottle and carry it around till it's finished. Sometimes he mixes Diet Coke with the Malibu. The rest of us drink tequila — cheap, gritty tequila from a dusty bottle. Carrie mixes it with cheap, syrupy margarita mix. We have less mix than tequila, so she makes em strong. One of us re-breaks the garage opener.

Things start to go downhill when Danielle and Carrie dare me to tuck my dick and balls between my legs and run around the back yard naked, which sounds like a terrific idea to me. My exhibition leads to a competition — who's willing to get the most naked? Jake will not be outdone. His competitive nature kicks in, and soon enough, he's completely naked, dancing in a circle on Rebecca's back deck. Carrie dares me to kiss Will, and I think I might have regained the lead until I look over at Jake. Carrie voices some idea that she's winning, that we get points per couple instead of per person, but no. No fucking way. I earned my points. Danielle earned hers. No way Carrie's latching onto Jake's exhibitionism for a free ride to victory. We all vote her last place, tied with Lara. Jake is in the lead, trailed by me, Danielle, and Will, in that order.

Lightning scares us back into the house. Since there's really no more naked to get, things deteriorate into a truth-or-dare game in the living room:

"Show Carrie your asshole."
"Get completely naked and jump over Will."

---

* Unless you are *named* Thong, as are certain East Asian students.

Soon enough we give up on the game. I think. For all I know we could have played for hours, but the last thing I remember is jumping over Will. After that point, the timeline just doesn't seem to work. I remember us getting dressed, watching TV. Everyone except Will. It seems like he was missing forever, like the rest of us sat downstairs and watched sitcoms for hours. Eventually Jake says "Where's Will?" and almost instantly we hear this rush of water right over our heads.

"Is he taking a shower?"

He isn't.

I run upstairs and hear him muttering, whimpering.

"Open the door!"

"Guys only."

"Ok. It's just me. Open the door!"

Will is in his white Fruit-of-the-Loom underwear. He's been crying and his mouth and teeth are full of blood. "God, are you ok?"

"It's just my thumb. I cut it and I've been sucking on it."

"What the fuck did you do?"

"I broke the toilet. I was masturbating. I was jerking off and I cracked it. I pushed back against the tank and it cracked."

"Fuck."

"I know. I'm sorry."

"Get some towels!"

"I tried to make it stop. Jesus, what's wrong with me?"

"Nothing. You're fine."

"I broke the toilet whackin off. That's not normal."

"Sure it is."

"Have you ever done it?"

Will balls himself up in a corner of the bedroom while the rest of us try to keep as much water as possible upstairs and as much ceiling as possible downstairs. Jake had the foresight to move all the electronic equipment — TV, VCR, answering machine — out of the room and to pull all the furniture out from underneath the path of the water. Now there are two giant sagging circles in the plaster. They're cracking along the edges and letting more water through. Danielle and Lara grab two buckets from outside and pull extra dog bowls and pots and pans from the cabinets. I pull a chair beside Carrie, who's on the edge of the couch trying to hold up the ceiling with her hands and a bath towel. "Motherfucker."

"Should we call Rebecca?"

"She's in DC for her dad's funeral. Just call a plumber."

Lara's already on top of it, back and forth from the phone and trying to comfort Will, who has locked himself in the bedroom upstairs. "Will says he'll pay for it."

"Ok."

"How much do you think a plumber charges at 3 AM on a Saturday?"

Repairmen laugh when she mentions that we're house sitting. She wakes them up, shops around calling not only Rebecca's usual plumber, but most of the others in the area. "No, it's Lara. L-A-R..." Will is whimpering in a corner upstairs, but the rest of us decide he wins tonight. Nobody can beat this.

Lara maintains control of the situation. She comforts Will, assures him he isn't a deviant. She assesses the damage. We're in a mad scramble to clean it all up before Rebecca returns tomorrow afternoon. Lara buys a fan and we aim it at the ceiling in hopes of drying out what plaster is left. We drape the rug across two chairs, aim the fan at that. We have faith in the fan.

Will follows through on his offer to pay for the damage — a blank check. We settle on a plumber who convinces us to wait til morning because even he can't bear to charge us his weekend rates. Speed is our main concern, and he assures us he can be here by 9 o'clock, finished and out the door by 12:30 — which will leave us approximately half an hour to mop, reposition the furniture, and compose some sort of note to explain all this.

"What should we tell Rebecca?"

"I say as little as possible."

"Do we really have to say anything? I mean, it's all back to normal now."

"I think she'll notice it's a different toilet."

"Yeah. The guy said hers was 27 years old. They don't even make that kind anymore."

"She might even be happy to get a new toilet."

"So ... Dear Rebecca, there was a slight accident ...."

"Please don't tell her everything. She is my doctor."

"Maybe we should just wrap a bow around it — *Welcome Home! Sorry Your Dad Died.*"

Either way we explain it, I know it's the end. Even a Buddhist holistic medicine specialist can only have so much patience and tolerance for us inadvertently wrecking her house. And even if she does invite us back, the damage level seems to escalate so much every time we house sit that I'm afraid to find out what might go next. Sniper is not in the best of health. Danielle and I both pay absolute attention to the dogs for the rest of our stay. We're always extremely careful with them anyway — putting their special shock collars on before we let them run in the yard, giving Sniper his special senior food and making sure the other two don't steal it before he can eat — but now when they sleep we watch them to make sure they breathe.

Nine

I heard the call for volunteers from Will. The Billy Graham Crusade is coming to town, and they need 1,000 volunteers. I had seen the announcements all over town: on billboards and sides of buildings and buses — "God only knows how it may change your life." Will tracked down an online application for me at work while he was supposed to be teaching blind people to use a computer.

Two weeks later, I am an official Billy Graham Crusade Volunteer. I listen in as local newscasters interview the crusade's organizers:

"How does Dr. Graham prepare for his sermon at an event like this?"

"Well, about twenty minutes before we begin, he gets all prayful."

Prayful is funny enough on its own, but at first I thought they said "playful." Like he's running around backstage tickling everybody.

As far as my own preparation for the event, I used Photoshop to splice together pictures of Dr. Graham and a corndog, creating this flyer:

The Billy Graham Corndog

"Heaven on a Stick"

The Billy Graham Corndog. Imaginary? Yes. Believable? We'll see. "It looks more like a chicken leg," Will says. But a Billy Graham chicken leg? What fucking sense does that make?

The volunteers bow their heads for an opening prayer. I keep my eyes open just like I used to do in church when I was a kid, looking around to see who else had their eyes open, watching people mouth their own prayers, trying to read their lips. I feel a little conflicted. I only pray when I want something bad not to happen, and here I am outnumbered by so many people who believe, who want me to believe. When you're passionate about something, it's natural to want it to spread, even when it comes off as obnoxious. But this — Billy Graham is all about show. It isn't a true religious experience, with its giant billboards and ads on the sides of buses. This is religion as corporation, as spectacle. It's a crusade, for God's sake. The crusade leaders prayed for good weather — not just that it wouldn't rain during the services, but for very specific conditions. "Let this weekend be mild, Lord, and not overly sunny." After prayer, they passed around the collection bucket. They actually called it that — a bucket. I guess when your goal is two million dollars you don't have time to mess around with something as small as a collection plate. "I know you volunteers have given us a most precious gift, which is your time. But if you have some coins, or five or ten dollars in your pockets, please give us that gift as well."

God responds with a downpour. Inside the stadium, I'm surrounded by 30,000 Christians in Papa John's ponchos sold there on the spot. Some of the more DIY Christians wear garbage bags with arm holes cut out, or brave the storm with simple plastic grocery bags on their heads. It's a happy crowd. I've been in so many crowds that I've become a pretty good judge of their character, and this one has a positive energy, like the crowd at the Del the Funky Homosapien show in Cincinnati last summer. He was sicker than I'd ever seen anyone on stage, sick to the point that he held a styrofoam cup and spit mucus into it between verses, sick to the point that he went into dry heaves before "Catch a Bad One." That sick, but he didn't cancel. He came out and put every ounce of his medicated energy into the show. And everyone in the audience appreciated it. Just like them, these Billy Graham followers are here expecting positive things to happen. They're here to have a good time.

I stake out a spot near the entrance to hand out flyers. Old people give a goodnatured chuckle. I'm not sure if that means they believe in the corndogs and are amused by their novelty, or if they know it's all pretend, but are taking the prank well. Slowly I start to realize though, that some people are completely accepting. My official volunteer badge gives me some credibility, and I give away each flyer with a smile. "Have you folks gotten one of these?"

"God bless you for working," they say.

My fingers are numb and clumsy from peeling each flier from the stack, and my feet are tired from moving from place to place. I can't stay situated too long because I know there are security cameras following my every move. I'm sure they have a whole staff to watch out for suspicious characters and false corndog information. The stadium is really filling up by this point as the time gets closer to Graham's sermon, and I'm giving away fliers like crazy. I hand them off quickly and look up to see members of the choir, stadium officials, all come through the line with their hands out to receive a flyer.

But I'm overwhelmed by the size of this crowd — out-of-breath and feeling like I can have no effect on this many people. Then it happens — I actually overhear a concession cashier say "No Sir we don't have that corndog. We're more of a pizza stand."

It's working! I start to realize that people want to believe. Just like with God, they want to believe in the Billy Graham Corndog on blind faith, but they want to find it too, to prove to themselves that it's there.

Only one person tonight tries to call me on the joke. In the middle of the usual god-bless-yous and warm reactions, a woman suddenly stomps back to me waving her flyer. She looks at me with pity and I toss off the rest in my hand and move on. Someone's onto me and I can sense it in the congregation spreading like wildfire. They wanted to believe, but as soon as someone pointed me out for a heretic, they want to converge upon me. They all want not to believe.

I'm running low on flyers at this point and I'm tired from the effort, so I make my way to the railing along the very back corner of the stadium seating. Above everyone, looking down on them in their seats, on the choir, on the platform where Billy Graham will speak, I feel good. There's some sort of kind spirit here, whether it's God, Billy Graham, Del the Funky Homosapien, whatever you want to call it. There's something, and I'm glad I got to experience it.

I see a large retarded boy wheel in his ancient mother in a wheelchair, almost losing control going down the wet slope to the lower level. I see two metalhead guys in the front row wearing drugged-out grins. I watch all this leaning over the railing for almost 20 minutes, and then with my guilty conscience I leave before the service begins.

On my way out of the stadium, I am the only one walking away from the crusade. Everyone else is moving toward it. Families come in together — 16-year-old boys with mohawks and Dead Kennedys t-shirts led by their mothers, but looking smug, knowing the message won't get to them. As I make my way past the throng, the rain is tapering off. I look back and see the sun and blue sky directly above the stadium, or maybe more to the left, over the pasta factory.

Ten

Danielle and I have never spent a night apart. In almost six years of marriage, we have kept the streak alive. The longer it goes, the more important it seems to us, and the more we brag about it to people. And now I'm expected to go to a weekend team-building retreat with the English Department. I never thought it would end this way.

First of all, it's the weekend. Second, it's a team-building retreat. One of the main reasons to work at a university is to keep away from business culture and business jargon, and there it is, creeping in. Let's talk about being proactive and assess our productivity. Let's go on a team-building retreat, and let's hold a series of meetings to plan that team-building retreat. The department chair places an oversized sketchbook on an easel and uncaps a bright purple Sharpie to keep track of our suggestions about how to make this weekend the most productive. The only good thing about group brainstorming, which is how we spend most of our meetings, is that the department chair has to write down everything we say, including my comment that I don't like the idea of retreating from our workplace so that we can get more work done.

I'm proud of this comment. It's one of the first things I've said in a meeting and after some hesitation and sighing it is written in purple at the bottom of the sketchpad. This is the kind of comment I am not supposed to make as a Lecturer. I'm supposed to fear and respect the tenured professors and vote the way they vote. This is the system. The tenure system is based on fear, and young assistant professors know that they have to play by the rules if they want to get tenure and become grouchy and untouchable. But as a Lecturer I can't get tenure, so I make my comment anyway, holding onto some shred of faith that it may change somebody's mind. But I can see what I've done. I have separated myself from the group. I have shown myself not to be a team player. And in the end, I am outvoted anyway.

Having already spoken up, it is easy enough for me to go the next logical step and refuse to go to the team-building retreat. The biggest part of it is spending one more night with Danielle and keeping our streak going, but I also think it's good to make clear this early into the job what I will and won't do. I won't go to team-building retreats. This act of resistance is small, but it makes me proud, and at the same time terrified.

The English Department's retreat was scheduled on the 23rd and 24th of the month, which conflicted with our monthly mini-anniversary. So we dedicate the weekend to blowing the money we earned house-sitting. It's been awhile since we did this. For Christmas the first year we were married we gave each other Dollar Store Shopping Sprees. On Christmas Eve I waited in the car while Danielle spent twenty dollars on mystery gifts, then we switched places. I got a tiny ceramic clown and a Darth Vader Pez dispenser. She got two wooden ducks and a butterfly magnet. One dollar per Christmas present and we still have that stuff five years later, although the heads have broken off the clown and one of the ducks.

This is our 70-month anniversary, and the streak will not be broken. We will not spend a night apart. Danielle is like an anchor for me. She backs up all my decisions, stupid or not, and she brings me back from taking myself too seriously. She makes me feel like I belong somewhere. I hope I make her feel the same way. The worst thing about working is all those hours spent away from her. She's the only person I can imagine spending 70 months with and still feeling like this.

I get tired of other people so quickly. Even after I was shown the light at the Billy Graham convention, I am not a joiner. I hate team sports and I don't like groups. A lot of people fear public speaking, but I don't mind speaking in front of a group. I just hate speaking within one. Most of my life I've had one or two close friends, and eventually dropped them to move on to another close friend or two. I have never felt like a part of anything. This is probably something I should work on. It's something I've been trying to work on. After this anniversary celebration, I'm going to the Underground Publishing Conference to meet other people who put out their own books. I want to check out the competition. Danielle wants to go bowling with some anarchists.

The Underground Publishing Conference in Bowling Green, Ohio is less of a conference and more like a festival. There are presentations and discussions scheduled all day, half of them about the self-publishing and zine-making processes and the other half about politics and life skills, like Home Ec for Hobos. There's music and performance art and the whole thing is capped off with a bowling party. But the real information is in the room with hundreds of people sitting at folding tables behind stacks of stories and essays and interviews that they wrote and stapled together. This is the scene I've been looking for. These are my people.

There was a time I wanted nothing more than to get my books out legitimately. I wrote a novel when I was nineteen and I sent it everywhere. Danielle typed careful address labels and we mailed them to agents and small literary presses. When there were no takers, I put it out myself. I didn't even have time for discouragement because I threw myself right into making books. I used posterboard for the covers and figured out ways to scam free copies from Kinko's. Danielle helped me make around two hundred of them, each one pressed between stacks of old textbooks and stuck together with a hot glue gun. I still have burn scars on my fingers.

At the time, I had no idea other people were doing it, and that there was information out there about how to do it. I didn't know there was any kind of community of people who did this stuff. And now that I see so many homemade books and zines in one room, I feel good that I'm part of something, and at the same time bad that my idea wasn't as unique as I thought it was. I learned from reading other people's zines that putting two staples down the spine is much faster and much less painful than using a glue gun, so that's what I did with *El Cumpleanos de Paco*. The staple-binding makes it look more like a zine than a novel, which led that Icelandic reviewer to call it "not a novel." I tried to coin the term "zine-fried novel" like "chicken-fried steak," but it didn't catch on.

Everyone here is taking notes, considering how they'll write about the experience in their zines: "My Trip to the Zine Conference." You can see their minds working, watching for details to include. I'm no different. The room is filled with underground writers and publishers, cartoonists, filmmakers, activists, zine distributors, punks, a pair of honest-to-God trainyard hobos from the Northwest — all coming together to talk about their projects and hear about everyone else's — anarchists, gypsies, activists, kids who have been on the road for years. The whole place smells like body odor and vegan farts.

After we get signed in, a barefoot, dreadlocked girl wearing overalls runs into the building excited. "There's a truck outside full of stuff from the dumpster!" The semester has just ended here at Bowling

Green State University. The dorms have emptied and students going home have left behind whatever wouldn't fit in their cars. The message sinks in and everyone runs outside. People picking through boxes and trash bags, smelling food and checking the expiration date to see if it's still edible. Half-empty boxes of corn flakes, ramen noodles and some weird candy from Mexico, some kind of tamarind-flavored goo in a plastic, rocket-shaped squeezer. Everyone has to try it, but only one of us seems to like it — this really happy, dirty, hobo-looking guy who announces, "If anyone finds a planner, I want it."

There's pottery everywhere. Someone tells us that Bowling Green is known for its pottery program, so these are quality projects people abandoned at the end of the semester. Danielle finds two ceramic mugs, a half-used notebook, and a planner for the guy who wants one. What does a guy like him write in his planner anyway?

Look through dumpsters.
Hitch ride to next town.
4 PM: Bring down the system.

He's wearing clothes he found for a dollar in thrift stores or for free in garbage cans, and the planner Danielle finds for him is a Ralph Lauren designer model which might have been thrown out by a sorority girl. He seems genuinely excited to get it.

I find a beer funnel. Now I can start my own fraternity.

Back inside, people set up tables to showcase their zines and comics and homemade t-shirts and videos. These are traded freely between tables, handed away in person or mailed across the world in exchange for a few stamps — this giant room full of creativity and everything's under three dollars. Here's where writing is alive. So many people not working, walking away from the whole system of having a job to devote their time to writing zines, to documenting their lives and their causes in handmade publications with names like *Xerox Debt*, and *32 Pages, Lovingly Bound With Twine*. People making films, running distros — those may impress me the most because distribution is such a mystery to me. Even more so to Jake, I guess. I don't remember where he read it, a flyer for the conference maybe, but he thought it said "bistros." "Learn how to run your own bistro." Like all these anarchist kids are opening posh restaurants. Distribution for me is dropping stacks of free books in coffee shops and laundromats. I go to workshops this weekend on DIY touring and collective distribution. I'm here to see if there's a better system.

Are people throwing my books away? I'm haunted by this possibility. My biggest fear is that instead of appreciating them as free, people disregard them because they don't cost anything. That they never get read, they never get passed on like I ask on the back cover — "When you get tired of this book, please give it to someone else." I'm afraid they're getting swept under tables, thrown away with piles of napkins at the end of the night. But the ones that are rescued — I watched a bartender sitting in a booth by himself two nights in a row at Cahoots, reading *El Cumpleanos de Paco* and smiling — never mind that two nights later I saw what might have been the same copy of the book get kicked around on the floor of that same bar. And here at UPC I meet a kid named Greg who found my book in a shop in Maryland.

But I want more. As inspiring as this conference is, it's defeating at the same time. So many people doing so much cool stuff that it makes mine feel insignificant. I attend some informative sessions on how to bind your own books, how to live for free, run your car off vegetable fuel, hop trains, juggle fire in the street for money, and form a self-supporting vegetarian farming community. At night they open the doors of the historic Clazel Theater for a gypsy performance troupe — inside, a guy on stilts leading another, shorter, guy around by a chain as he hands us small sheets of paper and screams "Give us your dreams!" I don't know whether he means dreams like when we're asleep or dreams like our aspirations. Either way, what everyone writes down is later burned in a coffee can along with three pubic hairs plucked right there on stage.

When everyone is seated, the performers suspend a white sheet from the stage rigging and position a spotlight behind it. The action on stage distracts us from the naked man creeping his way from the back of the theater. He's covered in a white powder that makes him look ghostly, and he dives under one row to resurface in another one, popping up between people's legs, stopping at our row to show me a Polaroid snapshot of a random family. He never speaks, but there's a real sense of urgency about it. Later that night Danielle notices a penis-shaped smudge of white powder on my shoulder.

The ghost man makes it to the stage and disappears into silhouette behind the sheet. He dances for us, joined by other members of the troupe, who appear out of nowhere and disappear just as quickly by moving into or out of the spotlight's beam. The naked ghost is left alone on stage until a second figure, with devil horns and tail, appears and jabs him with a pitchfork with WORK forged into the handle.

I'm so fascinated by what I see here that I go to the gypsies' informational session, which consists mostly of tips for hitchhiking safely and hopping trains without getting your feet cut off. There are diagrams drawn by Sharpie on an oversized sketchbook. The conference program asked us to steal something from an appropriate source and bring it to share, but the take is limited — one ball of yellow yarn and half a pack of organic Fig Newtons found in the dumpster. We were supposed to get free wine, but the gypsies had drunk it all.

Hitching, train hopping, food gathering, starting your own carnival troupe . . . there's so much to cover it can't all fit into a one-hour session. It's exciting, but then we start brainstorming. An anarchist girl in the front raises her hand and suggests we make a list of topics people are interested in and then rank them by popularity.

Eleven

Summer is winding down. Danielle's seasonal job at the zoo is coming to a close, and I'm working on a new syllabus and preparing to enter the PhD program at the University of Louisville. By this point in the summer I'm usually bored with whatever I've been doing, but still dreading the fall. But this summer I'm ready. I'm actually excited about getting back to teaching and taking classes.

But there are some loose ends to wrap up.

Technically, I'm sure I'm fired by this point. It's been over a month since Action World has seen me, since I ran off and left the Big Rigs without an operator. But I have two things going for me — my knowledge that the arcade is in a perpetual cycle of training, and the fact that my uniform still identifies me as an employee. My plan is to walk up to a random ride operator, one I've never worked with before, and introduce myself as their new trainee. One final appearance at Action World. Then I'm ready for the fall.

I drop Danielle off at the zoo and drive across the river to Indiana. The only problem with this final appearance idea is that I have some quarters, and on my way to the Action World manager's office, I am drawn to the Supershoot machine. After those few quarters are gone, I have some dollar bills that I change, but my whole game is off. I don't know how to explain it. Maybe I'm just out of practice. This early in the morning, though, I am the only customer in Action World. The first time Barbara the manager walks past, she pauses at the sight of me in my uniform, almost like she's about to tell me I can't play games on duty. But she shakes her head and walks away.

I take the few tickets I earned from my disappointing Supershoot games and trade them for one tiny Dixie cup of grape soda and one giant purple Crazy Straw. Now, I am ready for work.

I walk into Barbara's office with a swagger, sipping from my thimble-sized cup with a twelve-inch twisting purple straw. Former coworkers stare at me with slight recognition and confusion as to what I'm doing here. The assistant manager, particularly, is surprised. Or maybe her expression is more bewildered annoyance. "Hi guys. What ride am I working today?"

Barbara shakes her head.

I had expected more of a reaction. The Barbara I met at the beginning of the summer yelled at employees for trading shifts without running it past her first — "You'll work when *I* say you'll work!" — but at the end of the summer here I am, the employee who won't work when he's scheduled but who shows up randomly when he isn't. And what do I get? I get nothing but head-shaking and a facial expression like she feels almost sorry for me, sorry for all of us. I don't know if it's the shadows cast over her face by fluorescent mall-lighting, or maybe self-reflection prompted by my low score at Super-Shoot and the fact that this whole "final appearance" idea wasn't a very good one.

***

At my teaching job, my small act of resistance hasn't gotten much of a reaction either. The team-building retreat went as planned, even without me, and nobody even comments on the fact that I skipped it. But they look at me differently now, when I'm in line to make copies or borrowing quarters from the department coffee fund. I can see it. I'm the guy who didn't want to go camping with them.

And, they voted me chair and sole member of two committees that nobody wanted to do. That's what happens when you skip a meeting, I'm starting to figure out. You actually end up doing more work.

***

I've been thinking more about work and ambition, and I've been spending more time with friends who don't work at the university: my new friend Adam, who works at a comedy club, and my old friend Chad, who's one year away from becoming a doctor. Comedian and Surgeon may seem like opposite ends of the career spectrum, but they are both careers that require some planning and dedication. Adam is paying his dues hosting open mic nights and mopping up restrooms, just like Chad is paying his dues taking pulse rates and blood pressure. But Adam seems more excited about it.

I met Adam when we were both performing at Insomniacathon 2001 — 52 hours non-stop music, poetry, puppetry, juggling, et cetera. Adam was doing stand-up. I was reading stories and giving away free books. Adam seems nothing like a 26-year-old. Most people would say he has a childlike quality, but there's also something of an old man about him. He likes things quiet, and can't stand when parents bring young children to movies or restaurants. Adam is completely bald. He has a joke about it, about how people ask him if he's some kind of racist skinhead — "Let's face it. If a race war breaks out, neither side wants me." Adam is skinny and he wears tight striped shirts from vintage shops.

Adam works most weeks at the local comedy club, but he's starting to book shows out of town. Last week he did a guest set at a club in Nashville, Tennessee. Next week he goes to Appleton, Wisconsin, and then back down to Memphis. Backtracking is the downside to doing all his own booking and scheduling, but traveling is paying off. He just won the first round of the Midwest Joke-off, the rules of which probably require not making the obvious joke about the name of the competition.

Adam likes to walk down back alleys instead of streets. "It makes me feel like I'm in Europe." From the coffee shop we make our way down alleys to Tyler Park. We sit on the stone steps under the giant stone archway and watch kids play Red Butt, which I assumed was less game than chaos until Adam asks "Hey, what are you guys playing?" and a grubby kid said "Red Butt."

"Redbud?"

"Red *Butt*."

The game, as they explained it to us, is vicious. The objective has something to do with hurling tennis balls from one end of the archway to the other, and it goes on like that for a minute until someone misses a ball. Or maybe another player can steal your ball from you — I was never quite clear. But when you miss, you have to run as fast as you can and touch the wall before anyone else can hit it with a tennis ball. If they hit the wall before you touch it — this always happens — the game turns into a firing squad. You have to spread your legs and face the wall while everyone else bombards you with tennis balls. Some kids don't make it. It's like *Lord of the Flies*.

On the way out of the park we find a stray golf ball and Adam turns it into our own game — we kick it down the hill diagonally without letting it get away from us. It's a difficult game, on a different level than Red Butt. Adam's dream for next year is to perform at clubs five nights a week in exchange for a place to sleep and, if he's lucky, free drinks. He's auditioning for Star Search in Atlanta, may get to open for Emo Phillips in Milwaukee. It's hard work, but he's excited about it. He seems genuinely happy with his job.

❅ ❅ ❅

My friend Chad, future surgeon and former #12 Dungeon Master, is hosting a Warhammer game at his apartment, and I am invited. I've known Chad since seventh grade, and now he lives two buildings down from me, but we rarely see each other. So I go, even though his friends creep me out and I have no idea what Warhammer is.

Chad is as disappointed with medicine right now as Adam is enthusiastic about comedy. His schedule keeps him so subdued and sleepy when he gets home that his apartment feels like nobody lives there. There are moving boxes he still hasn't opened. His stereo isn't hooked up. He's lived here for five years.

Chad runs three to five miles every day, trains for mini-marathons, but broke his foot when I took him to an MXPX show. Skinned his knee on bulk trash day last year when Danielle and I found a ping-pong table in front of this fancy Victorian house a half-mile up the street and I enlisted him to help me carry it to my apartment at 2 AM. I had to drag him out of bed to help with the ping pong table, but he seemed as awake as he usually does. Chad always looks like he's halfway asleep, especially since he started med school. I don't think he has ever seen a movie all the way through. He'll invite you over to watch a movie, or even worse, out to a theater, and he's asleep before the previews are over.

Chad introduces me to his friend David, who looks like he'd always want to shake your hand. His dad is a doctor. So is his grandfather. So now he's going to be a doctor. David grew up in country clubs. He looks like a brown-haired Ken doll. People have described him as "all-American." But unlike most of Chad's friends, David and I get along really well. We're the only people there who don't know how to play Warhammer, which seems like Dungeons & Dragons played with tiny, expensive dolls. David, though, is committed to learning the game. He's studying the player's manuals while I marvel at the price tags on the bottoms of Chad's Warhammer figurines. I will soon realize that this is a key aspect of David's personality. He plays by the rules. When you play any kind of sport with him he knows all the actual techniques for how to hold a tennis racquet or how to keep score in ping-pong. He's had lessons in everything. I asked him about it once and he said, "Why do something if you're not going to be the best you can at it?" It's his dad's philosophy, but it's given David some well-rounded talents. He can skate backwards. He re-diagnosed my heart murmur in Chad's kitchen. It's crazy. He said he could replace my car stereo, but in the end I was left with a giant hole in the dashboard.

The reality seems to be sinking in for my friends that by this time next year, people can call them doctor. After the game and before Chad nodded off, I asked him if he'll use this power.

"I've thought about that, and it's like this — if you were going in for invasive surgery, would you really want to hear your doctor was some guy named Chad?"

David still can't picture himself as a doctor. "I'm way more into art and music and stuff. But sometimes you have to go where the money is."

❊❊❊

When I told David about my adventures at Action World he laughed, but he didn't quite get the joke. "Why are you doing this?" It was a good question. Like with most things that seem truly fun to do, there wasn't much of a point to it. I started to explain all my stock reasons: refusing to be defined by my job title, refusing to be limited by it. Undermining the sanctity of the uniform and the schedule, the authority of the boss. But none of it came out right. "You just want to rebel against something."

And maybe David's right in a way, but really there's nothing wrong with that, not if I have something specific to rebel against. The problem is, I keep losing my focus. The end of this summer has been lazy. July's been a waste. I've spent some time on writing and research and designing my syllabi for the fall semester, but most of my time has been empty. I sit inside all day while Danielle's at the zoo. I wake up every morning to write for two hours, stories about these jobs. But they feel stuck now, like I've lost momentum. I remember coming home after my first night at Action World and writing page after page, typing away non-stop. But then that excitement gave way to the equal portions of relief and defeat I felt when I stopped going to work, when the whole idea just made me tired.

The end of summer means the end of seasonal jobs until Christmas. I scour the classifieds and turn in applications halfheartedly, but none of it pans out, and I secretly wish for it not to. The oil change place wants experience. The courier service wants some sort of sense of direction — they hand me a written test with all these questions about where things are in Louisville. "What's the quickest route from Bluegrass Parkway to Main Street?" "What streets downtown run north to south?" I've lived in this town for almost nine years, and I have no sense of its geography. I even sneak out of the courier office to look up maps on the Internet, and I still can't figure it out. It's pathetic. I'm horrible with directions. There was also an opening for a carpet-cleaning technician at Stanley-Steemer, but I never found their headquarters. I tried to respond to an ad for a doorman, but there was nobody to let me in.

Everything I felt excited about at the beginning of the summer seems silly now, almost embarrassing. Am I distracting myself from something?

Twelve

In the early 70's, Studs Terkel interviewed hundreds of people about their jobs. His book *Working* is one of the most famous books about work in America. He talked to people from all different backgrounds and socioeconomic levels – from Bank CEO to steelworker to prostitute. He doesn't really add much of his own commentary, just turns on his tape recorder and lets people talk.

So I did my own little interviews with my friends, all white people in their 20s, two or three years out of college and most of us working there. I interviewed them on the front steps of my apartment building and at Mr. Gatti's FastFeast Buffet, surrounded by 100 screaming pre-school kids from a YMCA day camp. I borrowed a microcassette recorder and told everyone not to be too longwinded because I was going to have to transcribe it all myself. For three weeks, I taped and wrote questions and transcribed. Each interview included this same question:

Have you ever read Studs Terkel's Working?
Carrie: No.
Will: I don't think so. No, I haven't. Do you recommend it?
Jake: (picks up the book) Did you *buy* this?
David: No.
Danielle: I read two pages out of it.
Chad: No I haven't.
Adam: What?

I asked them about what they do at their jobs, and about their philosophy of working in general. Chad and David's insights on medical school. Carrie's downtrodden-but-inspired argument against the 40-hour work week. Danielle's zoo stories, Jake's remembrances of his high school job at McDonald's. It was solid material. Nothing spectacular, maybe . . . just solid.

And bulky. I transcribed over thirty pages of interviews. But what I want to salvage here are some of the more memorable moments. Like a highlights reel. Picture me on a crumbling concrete porch with Carrie. It's nighttime. There are crickets. Or sitting on the hardwood floor in Will's new apartment with the picture of Thomas Merton over the toilet. Lara fell asleep before I could interview her that night, so she's asleep here too. Or better yet, if you prefer, think of it as one big group conversation — all of us together at a party or something. Like one of those high school parties from a John Hughes movie at the rich kid's house with the high ceilings. Or maybe a fraternity house ... either way, the party's going on behind us — crazy scenes, people having fun, Lara sleeping — and we're all seated calmly around a small table, a card table maybe, a ping-pong table with the net removed! — just talking naturally. Nobody's being interviewed.

Picture yourself with us if you want to. You're invited. Jot down notes of your own insights about work, about anything you'd want to bring up, really. We're not tied to the whole work thing. Run them through in your mind til you've phrased them perfectly and they sound witty, but natural, not like you've had time to plan them. Oh yeah, and the scene behind us — it *is* a frat house, I've decided. It's rush week and in the background you see two overweight frat brothers, one with his shirt off, working together to tilt the keg hoping they can coax the last few sips out of it. It's a different pair of guys every few minutes, but they're all doing the same thing.

And if you're not feeling creative, just pick one of us and pretend you're the one saying the things he or she says. Most of my own questions and remarks are in italics, just like Studs Terkel uses. (And remember, it's all just the natural flow of conversation, not like it's been recorded and spliced together to form some kind of idealized, manufactured discussion.)

Adam

A book about jobs, about *odd* jobs? Or a book about working, like the philosophy of working? I guess I would probably want to know why people quit jobs. You know, why some people will just decide one day not to go in to work. Because I've always . . . obviously there's no way I'm going to just not show up for a job. It screws everyone else who's working that day, I mean your friends, or at least your coworkers. Doesn't mean that I haven't. I worked in a grocery store and I did that.

Danielle

I guess I argue with my bosses a lot. I don't like them. And if I think that they're too conservative or they look down on their employees and stuff like that I kind of challenge them. Probably the most fucked up thing I've ever done was yell at a boss for about half an hour and then quit. The only thing that I can remember saying to him is that nobody who's ever worked with him liked him.

Will

Will works at the American Printing House for the Blind: "Research assistant, which is the bottom rung of a whole classification that goes up to research scientist. There are a couple of those. They're old. So it'll take me at least 60 years to get up there if I stay. At least." His other co-workers include seeing-eye dogs with people names like Fred and Dave and Dana.

I hear Dana's name all the time. One of the project leaders walks through the hall with Dana and she has to tell Dana where to go, which completely defeats the purpose of a guide dog I would think. "Dana — left! Dana — right! Dana — straight!" Why don't they just put *you* on a leash, let you lead Dana around?

Carrie

So what's the story about working at Target and they made you do the thing with the hula-hoop?

It was Target University and they made us all go into this room and they gave us this big lecture about guest services and all that stuff and then they played "I'm So Excited" and they turned it up real loud and they made everyone get in a circle and hold hands and pass a hula hoop across their arms and over their heads without letting go of each other's hands. And they played all sorts of stupid games like that and I think made everyone feel very uncomfortable. A lot of touching the other employees. I just had the feeling that they wanted us to conform to this certain way of thinking, and they do, I mean, there's no doubt about it. They want you to represent Target. That's what they're after. So they're not looking for a bunch of individuals. They're looking for a bunch of people who look like Target. Represent what they think Target should represent. It's just like McDonald's. "Smiling Friendly Faces" and all that crap. It's the same thing all over again. Politeness rituals instead of actually helping people.

Chad

This is something that you and I have talked about in the past, but I think it would be really interesting to live in a society where once a year you could just change your job completely. So like 11 months out of the year you work at your regular job and then on that off month you go do something completely different. But um, that's probably an impracticality.

Yeah. I remember you bringing that up.

I remember you bringing it up, it seems.

I thought it was your idea.

I thought it was yours.° But I like it, all the same. I think it would probably give people a lot of respect for people who do things they don't do. I guess I perceive my job, or rather the job that I'll eventually have, as being like a fairly prestigious one, and it would be good to like make me not forget that there are people out there doing those other jobs like the nurse's aid that I pick on. It would probably do a lot to keep you humble. And it might do a little bit to help with job burnout as well, because you know that month coming up you get to leave the stresses of surgery behind to go be a cab driver or something.

And then the cab drivers become the doctors?

Danielle

I mean, it's a cop-out getting these easy jobs where nobody really expects you to do much of anything, but at the same time it's a little more interesting and a little more fun. I just always see that as something I could quit anytime that I wanted to. But once you get a career, it's like that's what you're supposed to be your entire life. A career is different than a job.

°It was Thomas More's idea. That's how they did things in *Utopia*.

Jake

First official job, I worked at McDonald's back home. My job was the dishwasher so that would be all right. I'd get big huge black garbage bags and put them on as pants and shirts and shit and then wash dishes for about two hours. But just screwing around with friends we'd have the tomato slicer, throw tomatoes at each other. Play hotcake frisbee. I used to make all kinds of weird shit. Like hotcakes I'd make as big as I could, make all kinds of other stuff and we'd melt Barbies in the fryer, put eggs in the fryer. Trey worked there then. Trey was my best friend and he was pretty much the manager so we just did whatever we wanted.

Adam

You ever get fired from a job?

No. I was let go at one point, but it was only because the guy I was working for died.

David

A few months ago, David did some work for medical school in a doctor's office in Danville, Kentucky. To spare him the expense of renting an apartment, the doctor offered to let him stay in an extra bedroom in his house. David spent most of his time studying in his room, and was never really sure how to relate to the doctor and his family. But he felt sorry for the family dog because it always seemed lonely and never got any attention. So one day he couldn't look at his textbooks any more, and he decided to take the dog out in the front yard and give it a massage. The dog was starved for affection anyway, and it must have loved the massage, or maybe David massaged a little too low on its belly, but when he turned to leave, the dog tackled him and started humping him energetically. He says nobody was home at the time, but Danielle and I like to imagine the whole family inside at the dinner table, watching this scene out their picture window.

So I had this dream that I was talking to a patient who was being rather belligerent and demanding, and was concerned about his condition. I was telling him what he *didn't* have. I forget what his complaint was — he might have had like a cold or something — he wanted to know what was going on, and I told him what he didn't have. "Well, you *don't* have a sprained ankle. . . you *don't* have syphilis . . . you *don't* have meningitis . . ." And I wasn't being sarcastic. I was just, I don't know, I was being pretty honest in the dream.

Basically everything we've learned has been multiple choice. And I feel like I may not know what's going on, but I can pick it out of a line-up. At the same time, while I might not be able to tell what's going on, I'm able to differentiate that from what it isn't.

Chad

Last fall I had the benefit of seeing a faceless man. Basically he was a diabetic guy and I guess that leaves him immuno-compromised and susceptible to certain infections that you or I wouldn't be suscep-tible to. And there's a particular fungal infection called mucormico-sis which he happened to come down with, and basically this fungus goes up your nose and basically eats your face. And so he had . . . kind of like from the base of his skull up was intact, so his brain was all there and his mandible was there. But he was missing his maxilla and nose and his eyes. And when I saw him, he was just sitting on a stretcher throwing a Coke down his hole.
So to speak.

Will

I always thought before I started working at the Printing House for the Blind that guide dogs were trained and they knew their job and they didn't play around when the harness was on. But it's crap cause they run around like puppies. They get lost and they shit on the floor. It's disgusting.

So who cleans up the shit?

Blind people do and it's fun. They don't know what they're grab-bing at. They pick up a cup and they think they've got the poop. "Hey I got it!" and there's like this big steaming pile of crap in the middle of the floor.

David

Every day I've been looking for a reason why I should really devote myself to this profession and being a doctor. I don't know. I've been pretty frustrated for the last three years. Of all the rotations, I never took a sick day. There was one day where I was thinking about dropping out of school, and I decided not to go in in the morning. I'd had it. I wanted to like drive to Canada and say fuck school, it's all bullshit. But I ended up going in that day.

Carrie

No longer works at Target, by the way. Now she's a secretary in the University of Louisville's College of Education and Human Development. She's been working a full-time schedule for six months as a temp, and for two weeks now as a full-time, official employee with health and dental insurance.

Last week I worked 37 and a half hours. Well, wait. Let's see. I took *one* day off, so then it's . . . not a whole day but like lunch til 5, so I only worked like three and a half hours that day. Two and a half I guess, and then Friday I took another half day off I guess. But that's unusual. Usually I work 37 and a half hours. I make copies, type syllabi and I move things ... physically. Furniture. You know, filing cabinets. Let's see, what else do I do? I work in databases . . . data entry type stuff. Um . . . mundane tasks!

Is that what it said on the job application?

Will

Jake: Have you ever worked in a mayonnaise factory?
Will: No. I would never work in a mayonnaise factory.
Danielle: Have you ever weaseled anybody out of something?
Will: As far as work goes?
Jake: Are you more upfront competitive or sneaky-ass competitive?
Will: I'm sneaky competitive.
Jake: Do you eat in the cafeteria there?
Will: No. I've never eaten in the cafeteria. The cafeteria smells like burnt insulation.
Jake: Have you ever found dog hair in your food?
Will: I have stepped on a dog once under the table. I dropped a piece of lettuce at a dinner once and the dog ate it and I was mad at it so I hit it.

Jake

I don't know. McDonald's was pretty fun. Some of the people I worked with — the older people I worked with — there was this old lady who worked the morning shift when I first started working mornings. My shift switched all the time. On the weekend I'd close and during the week sometimes I'd open over the summer. There was this old lady, like 80, who'd get really pissed off and go back into the freezer and just start throwing eggs into the freezer wall. But it kind of sucked because they fired her, because they found out she threw eggs into the wall.

So there were repercussions?

For her. I never got in trouble. But I never threw eggs in the freezer so there was no evidence. Usually if you see tomato slices people are just like "Aahh" [*the sound of people expressing how ordinary it is to see tomato slices on the floor, evidently*]

What about fried Barbies?

We threw those away. I don't think I ever got in trouble except the time I had a band-aid come off in a sandwich. Then I got in trouble for that. But they didn't fire me or anything, they were just like "next time you wear the band-aid, don't do that."

Danielle

There are two things that I really hate about work. There's how long people have to work. I really think that we should only have a 30-hour work week, and I think it'd be pretty easy to accomplish. And I think the biggest thing is just how they treat people like property. You just go in and you're totally ... you don't know the people who are your real bosses. The people high up. And they have no idea what your name is. All they know is that there's an employee somewhere that's supposed to do the job you're doing. And you can be fired at any moment and they don't care. Because they can replace you with anybody else.

Nothing ever ends like, every once in a while you think "When I quit here it's really gonna hurt them because, you know, I do a whole bunch of stuff and they're gonna realize it when I leave." But nothing ever changes when a person quits. They just get someone else, and there's really no glory in a job, I don't think. Unless if you've got like a hero job or something.

Like a superhero?

No, like a fireman or something like that. EMT or something.

Adam

The way to get your foot in the door at a comedy club is to go in there and kind of do all the shit work. Because that way when they say "Oh, somebody didn't show up, and we need somebody," then they'll tap you on the shoulder and say, "*You* — go up and do the show." So anyway, there's the comedy part, and then the time between doing comedy gigs, which is a lot of time and involves cleaning a lot of toilets.

When I first started off doing comedy, I was not making any money on stage. I was making maybe $100 a week, which sucks because when you're on stage you can't be doing your normal job, which usually I would make $175 a week cleaning up puke in the restroom.

Will

I'm on the continuous improvement committee and one of our recommendations is that we look at where the guide dogs poop. I'm not kidding, we had to write it up and present it to the big formal board. "We need a new dog poop area." It was great.

I'm part of one continuous improvement group. They're all over the building. There's one for the second floor, one for the fourth floor. There's two for educational research and there are tons back at the plant. So they all meet and then one representative from each of those groups goes to the BIG continuous improvement meeting. It's really just a bunch of bureaucratic nonsense so we can have free Cokes one day a month.

Chad

I don't know that everybody in medicine feels this way, but surgery in particular, or maybe even pediatric surgery, it's easy to look at your job as like a mission. Like something you kind of get up and go do every day as sort of like a war you wage. Be it against congenital anomalies in children or diseases that affect children, or against cancer, which is, you know, a major killer.

Carrie

I want to feel like there's a reason why I'm there, that it's got this purpose behind it. And the problem with my job right now is I just don't feel like there's a purpose. I have this feeling that I'm just there, sort of existentially. It doesn't really mean anything that I'm there. It's just something that I have to do and I don't understand why, other than, you know, just to survive.

That's why I want to be a librarian because at least that way I would feel like I was helping other people get information and learn things. Be able to be independent, not rely on systems for information, but rely on their own search, in their own way. And that's my complaint about work. It's not so much working that I hate; it's just the job that I'm in now. Working can be good. It just depends on what you're doing.

Adam

When I worked at Burger King I was sweeping the parking lot, which is another good job because when I was working there I looked forward to two things: I looked forward to loading the little burger pucks into the broiler, and then I would sit there and sing a song to myself. I would sing a Dream Theater song to myself because I knew the song was like seven minutes long, and every time I made it through the song I knew another seven minutes had passed. I could just sit there and load em and load em and load em. When it would slow down I would offer to go outside and sweep the parking lot. And I would kind of roam around and do a really good job. And I found a porn magazine out there one time. It had rained and it had dried, so here I am . . . first I didn't want my coworkers to see me looking through this magazine, so first I'm kind of sweeping it over behind stuff, trying to see what it is. I thought it might be one. Then I'm trying to nonchalantly brush or sweep open the pages. Then I swept open my pants . . .

David

Is it possible to love your work? Is there such a feeling as looking forward to work when you wake up in the morning? Because I don't think there is. I think that we get bored easily. And I think somebody needs to say, look, we just want to, you know, make your work worthwhile, so in the end-all result I guess you're somewhat happy. But you're not going to find total happiness in any one job.

I think Danielle was onto something when she said that the forty hour work-week is too long, and I think a lot of times a little variety would just be unbelievable. I think you've been mentioning that. You know, everybody can have their main job, but I mean it's so nice when you can go out and just do something totally random and irrelevant that doesn't affect your reputation or your résumé or anything like that. That would be great.

So what about the story about the lonely dog — do you want to tell that one? (Laughs) No.

Jake

Has moved on from McDonald's to managing a record store to his current position as an academic advisor at the University of Louisville.

I think I work just because ... I don't know. Part of it is a sense of responsibility, but the job I have now, part of it is because I like it. I like the social aspect of my job, because I don't really like to sit in my office and stare at a computer all day. I think part of it is a sense of responsibility to do certain things. I think part of it might be the way I was raised. I'm just saying that I was raised to just work and not ... not be lazy. When I'm sitting around ... I think this is the difference between me and Carrie or maybe me and you ... when I'm sitting around and I don't have anything to do like work, I don't have, a lot of times I don't have that creative energy to sit down and create something for me to do like write or draw or ...

. . . do lame interviews?

Lame interviews ... whatever .... Yeah, so I think it's a different mindset. My mindset is I sort of have to have something scheduled for me to do … to do it. And I don't mind going to work every day and sitting there and then coming home. I don't know. Even if I'm not really doing anything at work, because if I come home a lot of times I won't do anything there. During the day I don't feel like doing laundry or anything. It's something I'll do at night, but if I came home I'd expect myself to have like a job to do. I think I just work because I get up and I feel like I have to. Maybe that's it. I don't know. I've never thought about it. I've never thought about why I get up and work — I just do it. It may be because ... I don't know what I'd do otherwise.

Carrie

I think you should talk about how the workweek is too long, how it consumes too much of people's lives. I mean even when I work a seven hour day I come home and usually just bitch about work for a couple of hours afterwards. And by the time you get home and bitch about work for a few hours, and try and fix yourself something to eat, you might as well be going to work and then going to bed. For me right now I'm obsessed about how much I hate work. And it really just consumes my whole existence right now and I feel like I'm just going to work and then going to bed. And hating work constantly. I have dreams about … I have *nightmares* about it because I'm hating it so much. Just trying to get used to the fact that I'll be working a forty-hour week almost, probably for the rest of my life.

So would you sacrifice a certain amount of money for less work? Say you got a 25-hour work week, your same medical and dental benefits, but you had that percentage, like 50% of your pay. Would you accept that?

Definitely. I mean, what really sucks is that you can't get any benefits part-time. You just have no options. You have to work full time. If you want to have health benefits. If you want to go to the doctor when you're sick.

Fall Semester

Thirteen

I used to steal things for my own entertainment. I even got one of my friends into it for awhile. He had his own box of useless stolen goods at home. But then his mom found it and she burned it all. I never understood her logic with that. I mean, to teach him respect for other people's property, she sets a bunch of it on fire. We're lucky the real justice system doesn't work that way. "Good news, sir. We've found the man who stole your car and he's going to jail for a long time. Your car? No. We burned your car."

It was Adam who got me into the comedy business. I applied for one of the official ticket-taking, toilet-cleaning kind of work-your-way-up jobs like he has, but the manager never called me back. She was afraid I'd come in and write about everyone's personal life, the clinically-depressed underbelly of the Louisville comedy scene. So I got to skip past all the work and go straight to stage time at open mic. My first time up, Adam turned to me when they announced my name and said, "Don't make a joke about the lights."

"What?"

"It's going to be really bright up there, like blinding. You won't even be able to make out faces in the audience. But don't say something about it. That's what everyone does."

"Ok."

They started laughing as soon as I stepped onstage. I hadn't even opened my mouth yet. The laughter died down when I started to tell jokes.

Adam tells me it's a real talent to go up and get laughs on your appearance or facial expressions alone, and after the show was over maybe I could look at it that way too. But when I walked on stage I wasn't doing anything special. I wasn't going out of my way to look funny, but it was the biggest laugh I got all night.

125

✳ ✳ ✳

Adam and I look like brothers, according to a girl who works in the coffee shop, the one where they'll let us put comedy flyers in the back by the restroom, but not out in the open where anyone might see them. After we pay for our coffee, she changes her mind and now says that we *seem* like brothers. It's the end of summer and Bardstown Road is newly deserted, the arcade and youth center empty til later tonight. The kids will come out at night for a few more weeks until it gets colder and school starts to take its toll on their energy. We post comedy flyers on telephone poles, between photocopied sheets announcing the "Last Show!" of bands that started less than a year ago, and reunion shows from bands that broke up last month. We play Frogger across four lanes — hopping from coffee house to record store to arcade. The first dead leaves blow in the street.

The stink of Louisville in August creeps up from sewer vents. When it catches you off-guard it's the taste you recognize first, like a film on the roof of your mouth. We get burritos and I ask Adam the difference between an A-7 chord and an A-7 Major. He launches into this complex explanation of music theory, draws a full diagram on the back of his napkin and everything. But I was really just asking where you put your fingers. A new semester is starting and I'm taking Seminar in James Joyce at U of L and Beginning Guitar at IU Southwest — free tuition as part of my new full-time employee benefits. I'm taking these classes for a number of reasons.

Number one: two classes makes me officially half-time, which means that my student loans can go back into deferment for this semester and a six-month grace period following it. I'm doing it, I think, I am living out my dream. I think this briefly, until the student loan company reveals the clause that all six hours have to be at the same university. Dammit.

Number two: the thing that kills good teachers is that they forget how it feels to be a student. So I'm taking guitar to remember how it feels to learn something absolutely foreign to me, even at its most basic level, and I'm taking Joyce to remember how it feels to sit in a classroom for three hours listening to somebody talk.

Number three: I kind of miss being a student.

Nineteen days into August and I already want to wear long sleeves, buy new notebooks and ink pens for school. Fall is like spring to me. Leaves are dying but everything else seems new. Campus is one big picnic, free Cokes and cheeseburgers everywhere. *W.O.W.* — Week of Welcome. They play rap music in the bookstore. All this effort to make students think college will always be like this. Free condoms and deodorant from Campus Life, a free slice of pizza if you fill out a student credit card application or agree to switch your long distance to AT&T. My inability to grow suitable facial hair helps me blend in as a student so I can benefit from all this initial effort. But I've been around long enough to know it won't last. Next week it'll all be gone.

✿ ✿ ✿

I still buy trendy backpacks. It's my one crucial purchase as the fall semester begins, a new fashion accessory to convince myself time has progressed. Two weeks into fall, though, I'm losing faith. There are highlights — new courses, new students, new boxes of chalk in every classroom. But there are meetings, too. Program orientations, planning committees. We read minutes from the end of last spring. We pick up where we left off.

Next semester, they tell me. Next semester I will have an office — at least now I have my own desk in the big office, but it just isn't the same. IU Southwest is out of space. They've worked some construction money into the budget, but for now I'm a displaced worker. I carry everything — books, lesson plans, student papers in my trendy backpack, which I soon discover was designed to be more fashionable than sturdy. I'm a mobile unit. I read *Ulysses* at Comedy Caravan, respond to papers at Tyler Park. After class Adam asks if I want to go work on jokes or play miniature golf, and I say fuck yeah I want to play miniature golf, then that night I'm up til 3 AM planning classes, reading chapters for the next day.

Adam asked to sit in on two courses I'm teaching this semester, American Literature Since 1914 and Writing in the Arts & Sciences. Not completely ethical on my part I guess, but he already has his degree and these are just extra classes he's taking out of curiosity, I think, about what I do at work. It's not my best semester. I can't keep my mind on things. Just like fumbling over jokes on stage, I'll start into a description of some literary device and trail off about halfway through, completely forget where I'm going with it. I'm worried that it's all lost somewhere, lost in the swirl of PIN numbers, hip hop lyrics, and guitar chords. And I can see through to it until it really matters, and then it isn't there anymore.

In guitar class so far I've learned to play Sugar Pie, Honey Bun and a very half-ass Smells Like Teen Spirit. Playing at home with Danielle I feel pretty secure, but in class I feel like I'm always behind everyone else. Like whenever they switch chords I'm still thinking about it, planning the best way to maneuver my fingers. Adam says it takes awhile, that if I just keep playing it'll come to me. I guess he's right. I can already tell some improvement from before, when I didn't play at all.

My guitar instructor is one of those teachers who believe skills come in building blocks, like you have to perfectly understand things at their most basic structural level before you can do anything with them. If he taught writing, we'd spend all our time diagramming other people's sentences, mapping out subjects and predicates or determining where a semicolon could go. I want to skip past all that. I want it in its most functional form — here's how it makes noise, now go make some. Guitar class is teaching me things, but it just moves so painfully slowly. I tried to explain it to Adam and he offered a trade-off — I'll teach him Beat literature and he'll teach me punk guitar. I thought he was joking at first, but when I laughed I could tell it kind of hurt his feelings. I started to say something, but it didn't really seem like the kind of thing that would require an apology. So we sat there for a second, uncomfortable.

***

Is it weird hanging out with Adam after class? Yes, but not because of any teacher-student power dynamic or anything like that. Basically it feels like I'm second-guessing everything. Just like Adam coming off stage asks me what I thought of his new jokes, after class I ask Adam how he thought it went, what worked and what I should have done differently. He's the inside critic I always wanted, an actual student perspective on what kind of job I'm doing. Probably not as much fun for him, though. He sees the shaky uncertain side of teaching — I got frustrated fucking up explanations in class and he says it showed, although maybe it wouldn't have shown to someone who wasn't looking for it, like how Bragi and Michael taught me the wrong chord can sound right if you just make a face like you meant to play it.

This semester I feel conflicted, like my only truly good explanations and examples are the ones I use class after class. I finally know what I'm doing with teaching, but does that mean it all has to fall into a pattern? Just yesterday I caught myself using the exact same answer to questions about writing. It worked at 9 o'clock so I recycled it at 11. Both times, though, I was listening to myself and it sounded rehearsed, and distant. As different as I try to make every semester, things fall into patterns and by the end of the week I'm either numbed or exhausted. All this energy I've spent toward keeping things moving, making classes new and exciting … it's making me tired.

❊ ❊ ❊

Last weekend I went to see a movie, and these guys sitting behind me must have hated it. When we were leaving the theater I heard one of them say "Man, that was the gayest movie I ever saw!"

I don't know, though. The gayest movie I ever saw was probably Locker Room Studfest 2000, *or* Heavy into Marty, *or I don't know …* ManHole.

September 13, 2001. Two days after terrorism brings down the World Trade Center I'm onstage telling jokes about gay porn and cottage cheese. The laughs don't come easy. It's like putting me up against Nolan Ryan the second time I play baseball.

This technically is my third performance at Comedy Caravan, but it's the first one I've invited people to. Some comics work for years to hone their act, but for me it was two quick run-throughs on open mic night and I'm ready to invite the world.

This is Danielle's first time to see me do comedy. Seeing me on stage makes her nervous, which makes me nervous, so she stayed home my first few times out. But tonight she's here. So are my friends, and students — three of them sit at a corner table, with their gelled hair and baggy jeans, they are easy targets for comedians — "Nsync is here, everybody!" It's the after-hours experimental show — free Thursday night comedy at the club, and over two-thirds of the audience is people I invited. The emcee makes me wait til last so nobody leaves.

Tonight the club is open for the first time since the attacks, and everyone is ready to leave their houses, to tear themselves away from CNN and the daze that they've been in. The day it happened, I woke up late and rushed to campus, put on my belt walking through the parking lot. I was late for class, so I made up for it by walking in and getting right down to business, announcing some new assignment. It wasn't until halfway through class that somebody asked if I'd seen the news. We turned on the classroom television just in time to see the second tower fall, and I cancelled my classes, packed up my guitar, and went home. All I wanted to do was see Danielle. I had woken up with

129

that nauseous, anxious feeling that I get when I wake up late for work, and it still hasn't gone away.

One of tonight's other amateur comedians worked in a finance office for fifteen years until his wife died young. Then he quit his job and started spending five nights a week at the club, taking notes on other comedian's stage presence and delivery, and developing his own act. "I'm not surprised it's so packed in here tonight," he tells me. "Sometimes this is all you can do." Will, conspicuously absent tonight — probably worried that my set will consist of jokes about broken toilets — has spent the past forty-eight hours making Photoshop recreations of footage from 9-11. His best pieces parody the Noble Eagle, an image that circulated widely on the Internet, that hangs in most office windows on campus. The original overlays both an American flag and a bald eagle over a shot of the twin towers burning and crumbling. The eagle has a single tear in its eye.

In Will's versions, the eagle cries about something different: a character from a TV sitcom — Mr. Belvedere for instance — engulfed in smoke, or it is replaced with Mr. T stomping through the wreckage Godzilla-style. In Will's personal favorite, he has morphed a second, smaller picture of the bald eagle into the shot, so that we see a new eagle crying about the first eagle crying.

When I see them, I think *Jesus Christ, Will*, but it's how he deals with it.

❖❖❖

I was in Steak-N-Shake last summer, and you know, I wasn't eavesdropping or anything, but I could hear the guy at the next table order his food. "I'll get a steakburger ... a chocolate shake ... large order of fries . . . oh yeah, and uh, cottage cheese!*"*

Cottage cheese? He said it like it was the coolest thing on the menu.

But cottage cheese isn't cool. Not unless I've missed something.

But then after I thought about it, I decided maybe that's his whole thing. This guy has it all figured out. Whenever he does something lame or boring, he can make it sound cool just by saying it like it is.

I picture this guy in his everyday life, you know, hanging around with his friends:

"Yeah, you guys are gonna like my new girlfriend. She's over-weight."

"I like workin out at the gym with you guys. I find it homoerot-ic.*"*

"We're goin out to the bar after this? That's cool. You know I like my beer nonalcoholic.*"*

Adam clears gaming manuals off of his living room floor so I can sit down. "Hey! I was thinking for my paper for the research writing class, could I do a paper about this online game CounterStrike? Maybe a study of the dead chat — when you get killed you have to sit out til the next game, so everyone basically watches the game and trades this running commentary, but in the world of the game they're all dead, so it's like ghosts talking."
"Yeah, that sounds like it might work."
"But what could I say about it?"
This is where it gets weird, because I'm trying to be as encouraging as possible about writing and classes and everything, but at the same time I want to complain about how pointless it all feels to me right now. I took Beginning Guitar for fun, but I signed up for the Seminar in James Joyce as my first official class in the PhD program. I was excited about the class. I was excited about the prospect of becoming a real professor. But now all of it just seems like a distraction. I want to be at home with Danielle and our animals. I feel safe there. I feel like I can control things.
Student Adam asks me how I like *Ulysses,* but it's Friend Adam I respond to. "Man, it just seems like all this extra work that I don't really stand to gain that much from. I already have a job. I don't know why I think I need to work toward a better one." It was one of those statements that came out all wrong because I'd waited too long to talk about it. In my mind it had sounded like an important self-realization, one I might act on, one that rejects the whole system of climbing your whole life toward better job more money. But when I said it, it only sounded negative and defeating.
"So ultimately what do you want to do? I guess get a PhD and make more money?"
"I mean, yeah, I'd make more than I do now. And I could get

tenure."

"Oh yeah, *tenure*."

"But that's not really the reason. I'm interested in it. Every class I take has a point where I'm completely excited and into it. Just sometimes it seems so pointless. You ever feel that way about comedy?"

Adam gets quiet — I have shifted the topic of conversation back to him. He stares hard at his new stack of publicity photos. "By this time next year, I will be a full-time touring comedian."

I have depressed Adam. I try to redeem myself making jokes about essays on James Joyce that map out the physical trajectories of his characters or count the number of times the letter C is used in a particular chapter. But even that turns into complaining. It seems sad, I tell Adam, to think of these professors who have devoted their lives to studying Joyce, or the writing processes of first-year college students. It seems so empty. I picture them sitting in a library at night doing research, studying a subject most people don't care about. "It just seems like their entire lives turn into their jobs."

"What would be a better alternative?"

I have to think for a few seconds, maybe twenty. "Variety."

*　*　*

In the James Joyce Seminar, there are ten of us sitting around the long wooden graduate seminar table. We sit in the same seats every week. I sat somewhere different once and everyone commented on it. Tonight, though, I'm happy with my spot at the table. Directly in front of me someone has drawn graffiti in blue marker:

"I smoked and fucked on this table."

The Joyce professor is all about James Joyce. She has some kind of endowed chair position. That's what she's here to study, that's what she's here to teach: James Joyce. Three novels, a book of stories, and eight decades of literary critics trying to figure it out. I'm thinking about how some professors can get so caught up in their subjects that everything contemporary passes them by. I can't see past college sometimes, like Adam couldn't see past punk until he got out of it. But I just recoil into small periods of indifference and come back for more. As easy as it is to write off academics as bullshit, I know I'll never totally get away from it. I'll convince myself I'm trying to find a way to exist within it while still existing within everything else, to use it for what I want to, like the guy who smoked and fucked on this table. That's not what it's meant for exactly, but that's what he did with it, connected it to his own interests.

Professor Hamilton: Does anyone know what a parallax is? It's a measure of a heavenly body from two different points on the globe.
Joe: Yeah.

We talk about the stream of life and time in *Ulysses*, Leopold Bloom's desire for the past and lost youth, and all I can concentrate on is how I wanted to stay home with Danielle instead of coming to class tonight. Just thinking about last week and how so many people died at work, so many people woke up Tuesday morning and had hangovers, or didn't want to get out of bed or say goodbye to their wives or husbands for the day. They all considered calling in sick, almost even did it, but for whatever reason felt obligated to go to work anyway. Just like after Danielle and I had some ridiculous argument then made up tonight and she convinced me I should go to class instead of stay in bed with her, and for whatever reason I got up and drove to campus.

Professor Hamilton: Peristalsis, in ways, is the key to this chapter.
Stacy: P-E-R-I-S-T-A-L-S-I-S. Peristalsis.
Amy: P-E-R- . . .?
Christie: Is that where you can swallow things while you stand on your head?
Professor Hamilton: No. I don't know what that is.

❊ ❊ ❊

Outside our apartment, the only reminder of tragedy is our sad bent flagpole, empty since 9-11 when some high school kids stole it to fly from the back of their pickup truck.

Zoo season is over and all week Danielle watches TV, slow motion replays of airplanes crashing into buildings. She calls me at work every day, asking me to come home after I teach. I start skipping my guitar class to come home and play Dead Milkmen songs with Danielle. But this isn't enough to keep her mind occupied. She lays on the couch when I go to work. She eats the peanut butter and jelly sandwiches I make for her in the mornings.

After two weeks she's overloaded with TV terrorism images. "I really need to get a job."

Anxious to get out of the house, Danielle goes with me and Adam to Bloomington, first in a new string of out-of-town comedy shows. Adam finally has overstepped his manager and set up his own appearances. He asks us to go with him for support. We'll be trapped in his car so he can test out new material on us during the two-hour drive. "What was better — when I said I'd just come home from work, or when I said I'd just *got* home from work?"

It's Monday night comedy at Bear's Place. Outside the club, Adam introduces us to Jeff Caldwell, a comedian who's been on the road full-time for thirteen years — "And look where it's got me, same club I was playing back then."

"Jeff, this is Mickey, He teaches college and he's written a couple books. And Danielle is quite the college graduate herself."

"I signed up for a job as a temp this morning."

"Can't commit to things?" Jeff was well into a PhD program in engineering at Johns Hopkins University. He was preparing to write his dissertation, when one day he just stopped showing up. One year later he was a stand-up comedian.

Danielle is a temp, but not just any temp, a University of Louisville temp, sent from one office to the next as she's needed. Her first assignment starts Monday at the medical school.

Adam uses his pull to get us into the show for free, and to get us seats beside him and Jeff in the VIP area, which is three tables blocked off by a folding chair in the aisle and a sign that says Keep Out. Jeff drinks a free beer and asks about my classes. "So what are you teaching Adam?"

"Well we just finished reading Kurt Vonnegut."

"Which one?"

"*Slaughterhouse-Five*."

"Yeah!" Adam is excited about *Slaughterhouse-Five*. "Mickey's been teaching us about meta-fiction — historiographic meta-fiction and meta-narrative ..."

"Oh, I love a good meta-narrative. Sometimes I'll curl up by the fire ... just me and my meta-narrative." Jeff has the perfected delivery of a seasoned comedian. He can say anything and never come off smart-ass, just like he's extended a friendly invitation for you to laugh at yourself with him. I doubt I will ever master this skill.

Jeff tells us about a show he's been filming for ESPN 2. "I'm actually putting my degree in engineering to work — it's part of their new pitch for educational programming. I think they got in trouble for not offering anything of social value or something. But this airs at like 4:30 AM. I'm the host. What I do is explain physics and professional athletes come in to illustrate principles like bodies in motion or the laws of thermodynamics."

Adam's first show goes horribly. Like he told us, all his new jokes are going to have to suck a few times before he gets them right. He's trying to build a longer set so he can tour as a feature act rather than do guest sets or host. The one old joke he keeps in the act tonight — his funniest and most original — is ruined when a very drunk woman in the crowd somehow guesses the punch line and yells it out before Adam gets to it. There are two shows tonight, so he'll get a chance to rework things before he goes back up. He asks Jeff to analyze his set and point out weak spots and jokes that had potential, and while they go over performance notes, Danielle and I walk across the street to get coffee.

It would sound fitting for some reason if I had decided at this moment that I was finished with comedy, but it happened earlier, at no specific moment really, and for reasons I'm not sure I ever consciously thought about.

Fourteen

Like with most things, I continued to look for side jobs even though I didn't know why I was doing it. My energy for things had deteriorated into energy for the *next* thing, into this consistent impatience that left me sitting through everything — every class, every conversation — drumming my fingers across my knee in a NOFX rhythm waiting for whatever I was doing to end so I could be somewhere else. It was all nervous energy and no enjoyment from my experiences, just frustration that they were taking so long.

Tonight is my first shift at the Haunted Morgue. Halloween, the official October one, will be here in three weeks and this job gives me a jumpstart on celebrating. I remember when Danielle and I signed up to be haunted house characters back in July. We rushed to get our applications in before anyone else's. Not having any real acting experience, we hoped to get jobs based on enthusiasm:

Please List Any Special Skills Related to this Position

I celebrate Halloween two times a year!

Danielle is a mourner in the funeral parlor section of the Morgue. Her job is to use her wails of grief to distract visitors for a split second until the kid playing the corpse can bust through the lid of his coffin. I sit in a make-up chair for almost 45 minutes and then a second make-up woman tells me the first one did a shitty job and we start all over. I'm made up as "Dead Person" and am instructed to lie on a shelf in a dark room. The shelf people, we're called. I'm stationed here with three other actors: a high school junior named Steve and two very quiet girls that I guess are around his age. We introduce ourselves and wait in the dark. Steve tells us how he set up his own haunted house last year using animal parts from his uncle's butcher shop — "We had cow blood everywhere, pigs' heads on sticks lining the way to the porch ... it started to stink after a few days, but that made it even scarier."

Not sure what's expected of us, we try to get comfortable and settle in for the pre-opening night practice run. Tonight people walk through the Morgue with free passes and low expectations. But we still get a pep talk. The director approaches the haunted house as if it were some kind of Broadway production. He's painfully controlling of every aspect of the Morgue — uptight about every detail going the way he wants, but it's like he's making it up as he goes along. Before the show tonight, he gathered us all into the dressing room for instructions. "Tonight," he told us, "is sort of an ad-lib dress rehearsal. We may give you a script tomorrow night. But if we don't — we probably won't — try to just, you know, be scary." With that message and a quick demonstration of the effectiveness of "walking around real creepy," he sent us inside to our assigned positions.

Trapped in our shelves, Steve and the rest of us roll around trying to keep our keys out from under us and bony parts like elbows and pelvises away from the hard wood of the shelves, which are like a giant sturdy bookcase built into the wall. We debate for a few minutes about what is our role exactly. The shelves are in a very dark corner — probably the darkest in the haunted house, so we have a good element of fear by surprise already going for us. But are we dead? Undead? Some sort of shelved slaves? Who built these shelves and put us on them and why? The consensus is that we're weakened zombies, which for some reason leads us to the tactic of lying very still with our limbs dangling off at improbable angles uncomfortable for the living. When someone walks past us, we can let out moans or start kicking our feet against the shelf above us.

Each of us has a character name written on a strip of yellow legal paper we were handed before the show. There seems to be some kind of overall story to the haunted house that we were never let in on. In the first section of the morgue there's a prom, a car wreck, a funeral parlor — where Danielle is stationed, some sort of butcher shop, the Bloodbath, and an electro-shock room run by a mad doctor. Those are just the rooms we passed on our way to the shelves. We have no idea what's on the other side of us. We notice a Fifties theme to the character names. The other shelf people are Bobby Lee, Brenda Ann, and Betty Sue. I'm Dead Person. The director comes through and changes my name to Dead CEO, which still doesn't give me a lot to go on.

When the lights go out, it's our cue to stay in character and be ready to scare people at any moment. While we wait for the first group of people to come through, I try to come up with better haunted house themes, scarier character names like Ghost of Tupac, or Zombie Jesus. Steve, across from me on the third shelf, hooks his legs around a corner post and hangs his torso completely off the front of the shelf. He's the first thing customers will see as they round the corner, which should work great because he's scary enough on his own to take the attention off the rest of us so we can launch a surprise after-scare. Steve rolls his eyes back in his head and looks truly contorted and freaky. Since nobody else is talking, he maintains sort of a running monologue — "All my friends have nicknames. Like I know this guy Bacon. Somebody was talking about him one day — *have you guys seen Patrick?* I don't even know anybody named Patrick. I don't even know the guy's name."

Our faces have all been painted with a white base before the make-up people added on their personal touches like my green and gray splotches and the dusting of brown dirt all over my arms and neck — "Like you dug your way out of the grave!" the make-up woman told me, the same one whose left breast kept rubbing my nose while she applied some sort of silver goop to my hair. The total darkness of our corner is accented by the red glow coming from Dr. Shock's Lair, and it casts this eerie alien shadow over everyone's face.

Betty Sue, on the shelf underneath mine, bunches herself into a sort of fetal position bracing her legs against the back wall and drooping her head over the edge of her shelf. I twist around sideways, hanging half my body over the edge of my shelf so that one arm, one leg and my head dangle over the side toward Betty Sue. Our faces are a foot apart and we stare at each other with zombie eyes. Her head is cocked back so that I'm staring more at her chin than anything, but her eyes are completely empty. She blinks and swallows, but I never can hear her breathe. I notice the symmetry of her face, how it looked kind of off at first but is perfectly balanced and round, and there's this terrific oozing red wound in her temple.

Brenda Ann, the remaining shelf person, is absolutely still and silent the whole night. While the rest of us shift around, me pulling splinters out of the flesh of my leg or Steve wiping stage blood out of his eyes with a napkin — "fuck it *burns*!" — Brenda Ann remains stiff, staring at the shelf above her. Thirty minutes go by and we're still in the dark, waiting. I realize early on that my drooping body idea was a bad one. My neck aches and my leg's going to sleep. I slide further back into the shelf, toward the wall. How scary are weakened zombies anyway? Would pillows make them any less scary? Goddamn, it's taking forever for somebody to come through.

"... me and Patrick started this thing where anytime we see one of our friends we all tackle each other."

※ ※ ※

We find out later that the shelf people *were* supposed to be dead bodies. The director wants to reassign us — he decided against a pile of bloody corpses so soon after September 11th. So he adds more dead bloody rats and a second mad doctor, seals up the Ghost Dust because of the Anthrax connection. For the official opening night, I get transferred from the shelves to my new position as the Torturer. And that's what I say as people come through — "VicTIMS ... Victims for the Torturer!" I grab hold of a pipe overhead, a dusty motherfucker from this 160 year old basement turned haunted house, and I swing out over their heads, almost right in their faces, kicking at the chains and severed arms and legs suspended from the ceiling. I scream and do an evil laugh and swipe my plastic knife at them. There was also a sword, but I tripped over it and broke it.

Sean and Lauren work in the same room with me — they play my victims — and we have it timed perfectly. It's the best scare spot in the house. Sean's a long-haired emaciated Jesus-looking guy with a ripped black shirt and creepy eyes — man, he could play Zombie Jesus! He paces back and forth in this wire cage to my right. He's the first thing people see when they round our dark corner, and he's perfect. He leans against the wire and stares until they notice him, looks so spooky but so calm they freak out but instantly forget him and get distracted by these glow-in-the-dark mushrooms painted along the back wall. At that perfect moment, he springs from the back corner of the cage to the front, giving them a solid initial scare before they rush around the corner to get away from him, and Lauren and I bombard them. First with her shrieking for help from their right side, then with me jumping immediately out of the shadows to their left. Three scares in thirty seconds — we're a great team. I get the best scares when I hang from the wire of Sean's cage, in the back. People spot me at the same time they see Sean and assume I'm another, less spooky, prisoner caged up with him. By the time they round the corner, they've forgotten me, but there I am swinging from the ceiling, the motherfucking torturer. "Victims! VicTIMS!"

"Do *you* want to be my next victim?" I ask right in the face of a local news reporter.

"*No?*"

"Ok, just thought I'd ask."

She was leading a camera crew that was moving through way too slowly. As long as the line keeps moving, we have the scare pattern down, but when people hang around too long after the initial scare, I start to get more creative with my dialogue. Some frat guys come through and even though we — Lauren especially — scare the shit out of them, they try to gloss over the whole thing by standing around making jokes. They have a good laugh over our flashing red strobe light, psychedelic mushrooms on the wall, and the pulsing music coming from the speakers behind me. "What is this, a rave?"
"Yes, welcome to the torturer's rave party! Groove along with the torturer to your favorite techno hits."

The music coming out of the sound system is like trancy, repetitive loops of horror movie noises, some played backward to sound more spooky. *Boom boom Owshhh! Aaaawk! NO! No, don't! Shhrip ...Wrrrush Stabpph Errwwsshh*, the same thirty-second loop repeated all night, every night until Halloween. It was driving us insane. "Doesn't it sound like it says 'We must stab Elvis'?" Lauren asks. I agree that it does.

❊ ❊ ❊

Like anything, there's an art to scaring people. I've been practicing for this night since I was a kid, coming in early from second grade recess to hide under the teacher's desk and wait for the perfect moment to spring out, lying perfectly still under my sister's bed for as long as it took her to fall asleep. My friend Chris' mom almost pulled a gun on us one time. So tonight I was ready. I really got into it. Three straight hours of back-to-back scares and I'm feeling the effects of hanging from the dusty rails and pipes along the ceiling. I had blistered my left hand and then torn open the blister with a splinter in the back of Sean's cage. Real blood started to mix with the fake. I sliced open my right ankle on a chain, and banged my head into the wooden beam that supports the sound system. But I was still ready to frighten. A security guard came through warning us to sit still because he had two terrified little girls latched onto his legs. "No scare! No scare!" I thought he just meant those two, so when a few seconds later a new chain of little kids came through, I jump out terrifying as always. I realize after Sean and Lauren remain absolutely quiet that those kids were hugging each other like a unified shaking train. I told Lauren later that they looked like one really long little kid — like a centipede kid — followed up by a second, frowning, security guard.

They built the Morgue with all these secret passageways so that security could monitor everything and make it from spot to spot without having to walk all the way back through the building. One of them is stationed in our room because Lauren is chained onto this platform and probably looks tempting to grope. We're not allowed to touch customers, even if they touch us first, but I guess security has the right to retaliate. People are polite enough, though, and the situation never arises. The security guard is just a pair of creepy eyes staring out from the fake brick paneling. After eleven, the Morgue is empty and he comes out of his hiding spot.

Sean and Lauren unchain themselves and we all sit down on slave platforms or head-chopping blocks. Bloodbath Colin wanders over from his station and he and Lauren make plans to go out to a fancy restaurant still in their make-up. We're waiting for some kind of signal that we're closing down for the night, that the manager has given up on seeing more customers this early into October. We expect something to come over the loudspeaker, or the security guy's walkie talkie, but there's nothing. Then the power goes out. Lights, music, everything stops. Are we gonna be locked in here all night? Is it like that movie *Hell Week* where the fraternity sets up a haunted house and there turns out to be a real killer inside? Knowing there's no way any of us can find our way back out through the maze, we sit there, waiting for something bad to happen.

Fifteen

Danielle quit her job at the Haunted Morgue for a long-term temp assignment in an office at the medical school, where she works for an internal medicine specialist. During the day, she puts together PowerPoint slide shows and visual aids for presentations on chemical warfare. She assembles pictures of consumed children and Anthrax victims. She makes timelines about the progression of smallpox and the plague, and collects photos of kids burned by chemicals dropped from planes.

Working in the haunted morgue, we could have been made up as these people. We wait in line for make-up, sit in the chair for thirty minutes just to be sent home if there isn't enough of a crowd out front. Characters aren't paid for any of this time. No one clocks in until the ticket window opens. One week into the Halloween season, I'm finished. Danielle quit and now I want out. I've heard people say you should never get a job directly related to something you love to do — the kind of advice people give but never live by. I heard it when I started teaching, and I've always believed I can dodge it, that if I can help students develop their own energy for writing, it can all feed back into mine. I worry now, though, because of a few shaky weeks, if teaching is no longer new, and if once that energy dries up, there's no faking it. I wonder how long I could let it all drag out lifelessly. If I was miserable in this job, would I even realize it? Would I let myself fully admit it? Just like my last shift at the Haunted Morgue — the Torturer's lines seemed rehearsed and stagnant. Danielle agreed with me — new customers come through in two-minute intervals and it's exhausting after awhile to put all you've got into every scare. And the manager repositioning everyone at the last minute, or telling me I can't swing from the ceiling anymore because he's afraid I might kick someone and bring on a lawsuit, or asshole customers determined to prove to you just how un-scary you are — that stuff can kill your energy for anything. We got out just in time.

Danielle is glad to have a job to pull her away from television news, but I'm spending most of my time at home. I go in and I teach and I wait through office hours, but then I drive back across the river to Louisville and my apartment and my family. I've spent so much time away from them this year, at work and in class and out of town. Lately I feel really anxious about them when I'm not home. I'll be in class trying to remember if I fed them or not. I'll turn around halfway to campus because I get worried that I didn't shut the door to keep the cats out of the iguana's room. It's becoming a problem, but I feel like they're the only things I can keep safe.

❊ ❊ ❊

Blackie's FIV causes her to need teeth cleanings every six months. Her blood cell levels have been holding steady so far, but vets are never very optimistic about the rest of her life. The disease's effects are very similar to HIV, and so far Blackie's like the Magic Johnson of cats. Danielle and I have consulted with different vets and looked up all the FIV studies in the medical databases. Blackie stays on antibiotics on a pulse therapy schedule, which means every first week of the month Danielle and I have to trick her into taking her Antirobe twice a day. We researched alternative medicine for cats and added noni, Co-Q 10, and vitamin C to the mix, along with wheatgrass, which is the only supplement she eats willingly. Blackie is very patient with us, considering all the medicine we force into her, but Danielle and I still walk around with scratched-up arms and faces.

Taking care of a terminally-ill animal is tough. I don't mean to say it's tougher than taking care of a terminally-ill human, but there are two things that make it very different. First, the animal doesn't know it's sick. You have to make all the decisions about what medicines to force into its body and the whole time it's wondering what the hell your problem is. Second, somebody always brings up euthanasia, which doesn't even make sense in Blackie's case because aside from her bleeding gums, she shows no signs of being sick. And even though Danielle and I hold her down once a night and force pills down her throat, she also gets her run of the place. She controls this apartment. In her mind, she has no weakness. She still has so much furniture to destroy.

We've been paying so much attention to Blackie that when Danielle points out a spot on Decimus' tail I don't think much of it. We agree that it looks kind of scraped up and kinked, but we leave it at that. Iguanas are not the most elegant animals — Decimus has broken

146

three spikes off her back and rubbed one large spike off her head trying to crawl under the door of her room. We've seen more iguana X-
rays than most people can ever expect to. So the tail doesn't seem like
a big deal. "I'll call the vet in the morning," I say. Decimus is already
asleep, sprawled on top of the stuffed Komodo dragon Danielle bought
her at the zoo. "Showing him who's boss," Danielle says. So we turn off
the light, shut her door, and go to bed.

❋ ❋ ❋

I'm in the emergency room of the 24-hour animal hospital with
blood all over my shirt. Decimus has broken her tail. I should have paid
more attention yesterday. I called and made an appointment this morning but I didn't consider it a true emergency. I didn't realize she was
going to get tired of waiting and try to amputate it herself. When
Danielle got home tonight, Decimus had bitten halfway through the tip
of her tail. The only thing to keep her attention away from it was food
— she ate a half block of tofu and an entire bunch of collard greens.

Decimus seems fine, actually excited to be out of the house, but I'm
going insane. We're the least pressing case in the emergency room. In
the next room somebody's dog has been shot. Danielle and I hear the
people crying and the doctor describing the surgery and the little hope
they have of keeping the dog alive. It should put this tail injury into perspective, but I see it as a bad sign and it only makes me worry more.
Decimus is crawling in rapid circles around my neck and shoulders.
She tries to jump from me to the metal examination table four feet
away, misses and catches herself with one claw, scrambles up the side
of the counter, exploring everywhere. I haven't seen her this excited for
weeks.

The vet comes in, examines the tail, and makes a face. She says
they'll have to take off a small section of it, the bottom inch or so.
Simple operation. One snip. But they'll need to keep her overnight and
they ask what time they can call me in the morning. The operation
should be over by about four A.M. Call me tonight, I say.

There's no way I can sleep. Back home Danielle and I completely
disinfect Decimus' room to make sure she can recuperate in the most
sterile environment possible. The last time we cleaned her room, she
shit on the floor for weeks until the room smelled like it was hers again.
We stay up 'til 4 AM mopping and scrubbing everything she comes into
contact with — her Vita-lite, the giant stuffed Scooby Doo she uses to

climb up and down from her chair. We get rid of her favorite chair because Danielle questions if she might have caught her tail in one of the wheels. I try to find a suitable, safer replacement.

Decimus has her own room — she pretty much demanded it. When we first got her she wouldn't stay in her tank. We used to duct tape the lid shut to make sure she didn't tangle with the cats and she would bust through it. We could watch her. She'd jump from the bottom of the tank and bang her snout into the lid as many times as it took to break through the tape. Eventually she wore one of the spikes completely off the top of her nose.

She's tough. She can pull through a tail operation. Decimus has had a hard life. She was a second grade classroom pet before we got her — who knows what kind of hell those kids put her through as a baby iguana — and then lived in that house with the two huge dogs. She used to climb to the top of her tank and lure them over so she could swat them with her tail. I've seen her intimidate a dog, one time at the vet's office when a German Shepherd sniffed her carrier. We heard a hiss. The owner laughed at first — is that a kitten in there? Then the spiked tip of an iguana tail smacked his dog in the nose. She's not going to be able to do that anymore.

Decimus used to sit on top of my computer monitor while I wrote. She'd slowly make her way over, climb up my leg and across the keyboard and then fall asleep on top of the monitor, which was the closest thing to a sun-warmed rock that we seemed to have in the apartment. I used to take her for rides on my shoulder and when she felt the cold breeze from the air conditioning vents overhead, she'd open her mouth as wide as possible and stick her tongue out — I guess it's something like a dog sticking its head out a car window, but to us she looked supremely happy. We have pictures of it. It's heartwarming.

I feel a genuine connection to all three of our pets, but Decimus is the one I worry most about. She's the reason I became a vegetarian — that dream I had where somebody was trying to eat her. I've had so many nightmares about her. Danielle has too — these ongoing all-night scenarios where we have to rescue her from something and inevitably can't. Danielle dreamed once that our cats were lying around with their mouths open and Decimus kept trying to jump down their throats. It's crazy. I've talked to at least two people who told me they had dreams about Decimus after first meeting her — not always rescue dreams, sometimes the tables turn like Will's dream that she was chasing him through the jungle. See? That's what she's doing all day when she sits there so still and wise-looking. She's inserting herself into people's dreams.

Around 5 AM I get a call from the vet — Decimus is fine. She woke up from the anesthetic and ate an entire head of broccoli. Her phosphorous levels are way out of balance, but otherwise all the blood work looks good. High phosphorous can be a sign of kidney or liver problems, the vet says, but it could also be related to the fact that she's eaten four times her weight in vegetables in the past 9 hours. On the ride home I pull over four times because she's lying too still. She's still under sedation so her breathing is even harder to detect than usual. Does her makeshift plastic carrier let enough air in? Are the holes I made with the screwdriver big enough? I pull over in church parking lots, at a high school, by the side of the road. Is she OK? I open her carrier and jab her in the ribs to make sure she's breathing. To her, it seems like something a predator might do, so she reacts by playing dead. God, she can hold her breath forever.

I cancel my classes and stay home with her the next day. I play guitar for her. She likes slow songs built around C and F chords, strummed very lightly. I play "The Guitar Song" by Dead Milkmen and "Bankrupt on Sellin" by Modest Mouse. I cut up tangerines and more broccoli for her. For most of the day, we're inseparable. She licks her pineapple-flavored antibiotic from the dropper, eats all her vitamins. She gives little nods with her head and licks as she walks around, body language for feeling content or secure. Then, out of nowhere, she's sick of me. She stands up, puffs out her cheeks, and lunges at me all in one swift action. Iguana body language for "Get out."

At night I inadvertently terrorize her, easing open her door to make sure she's still breathing, to make sure her Repti-Lamp is giving off enough heat. But I can't tell from the door, so I sneak across the room and lean in closer and closer until her food-chain instincts kick in and she wakes up, again thinking I'm some sort of predator. She shoots off her chair and across the floor, trying to outrun me. She scrambles up the wall and behind the desk and tears the tiny bandage off the end of her tail. We can see her sort of wedged in between the back of the desk and the wall with her eyes bugged out, sides heaving from the scare. Danielle tells me I have to stop doing that.

I let her sleep while Danielle and I go for a walk. It's the first time this year that I can say it was truly cold. Danielle is talking about her new temp job, but I can't concentrate. This tail injury makes me realize I need to spend more time with Decimus, with all our pets. It's easier with cats. They have a few more centuries of domestication behind them. But Decimus, most of the time I don't think she wants that much direct contact with Danielle and me. I mean, she's glad to see us, even when we don't have food, but I think in her eyes we have more of an understood, but unspoken bond. And she doesn't completely trust us. Still, there have been some moments of complete and absolute connection. Last Christmas I played a board game with my younger sisters, one of those teenage girl games that ask you questions like this one — *What is the best moment of your life so far?* Mine was that day, that first day of spring after we got Decimus, and she noticed the birds singing. I raised the window and sat there beside her as she rubbed her face against the screen and her eyes brightened and she cocked her head like it was the first time she'd heard them. She put her hand on top of mine very gently and looked up at me saying Listen. Listen. And I did.

Sixteen

This fall has been dark and depressing. It's everything that summer was not. Summer ended with me wondering if I'm distracting myself from something, and I still haven't figured out what that is. I thought it might be my family, but no matter how much time I spend with my pets, I can't keep their gums from bleeding or their tails from breaking. I can't solve Danielle's fear and confusion about what she's going to do with the rest of her life. After the haunted house lost its luster, I've tried to step back from things, try to get some kind of perspective on myself. I write about James Joyce and write stories and plan for the classes I'm teaching, but my mind is not fully involved. These questions aren't easy, but instead of thinking more, I started working more. I haven't seen much of my friends in the past few weeks, and I'm starting to feel really-ly isolated. I went out to get a bagel this morning and when I started to speak, I was surprised to hear my own voice. I was getting worried about the future when I ran into two people from the past.

Nichole dropped my class months ago. Money reasons. Her job as a latenight security guard paid just enough to get her dropped from financial aid, but without financial aid she couldn't afford to pay for both rent and tuition. So she quit her job. She quit school. Now she's just killing time until next year, when she again will be poor enough to go to college.

Nichole is bored at home, so she makes the commute to IUS some days with her friend Robyn. While Robyn's in class, Nichole reads in the library, or listens to that guy play guitar — the guy who's always playing guitar — in front of the clock tower. When I come into the part-timers office today, she's sitting at my desk. "You're late for your office hours."

"I know..."

"Might as well skip 'em by this point." She makes some sense. I put up a post-it note and we go across the street to El Mariachi.

For a few weeks after she dropped, Nichole kept coming to class. She promised me a story about living in Madison, Indiana. River town, antiques town where all the kids get into drugs just to have something to do. I've never seen this paper, but today Nichole has an update. "I live in a house with three guys. First off, I'm not your mom. Second, keep your friends out of my room. I step over drunk, passed-out people all day. Nobody at the house does anything, and I mean *I* don't do anything *right now*, but I don't want to be like them. I don't even want to clean up after them."

El Mariachi has a newspaper clipping, framed, just inside the door that says " El Mariachi Serves it up as Good as its Competitors!" I feel a little bad for them, that this is the best compliment they've received. They should print it up on the napkins — "Comparable!" "Average!"

Nichole avoids salsa — "new piercing." She sticks out her tongue. "But you know what I'm saying? It's like this semester off has given me time to think. I used to feel trapped by it all, like it was just school-work-death. But what are the alternatives, sitting around drinking all day? I don't like working. I can't afford school. So what should I do?"

Jesus, I don't know. I pay for her bean burrito.

❖ ❖ ❖

Back on campus, someone is flipping me off from behind the tinted windshield of a red Oldsmobile. It is Shane. My old roommate. The guy who once tried to trade a camera to cover a car wreck, who stole a garbage can full of band clothes and left the Pixies without socks for the second half of their '91 tour. Shane was in a motorcycle accident when he was eighteen, so he drives with hand pedals. He taught me how to use them one night in the middle of a giant blizzard — we loaded his wheelchair into the back seat and spent hours sliding around in the empty parking lot at the mall. At this same mall, Shane used to graze in the supermarket without worry, dig into shelved cereal boxes for the prize or rip open bags of Funyuns in front of stock boys, eat all he wanted and then fold the bag over and shove it back on the shelf.

I lived with Shane my first year of college, the year before I met Danielle. There was no reason for Shane and me to become friends. He needed a roommate and I had $150 a month. Shane was twenty-four. I was eighteen, and out of my mom's house for the first time in my life. He became the twisted older brother I never had. He did everything from the start to assert his dominance. He took our one bedroom. I slept on a fifty-dollar mattress on the living room floor. When he woke up in the morning, I woke up. He would roll into the living room — my room — naked, at around six in the morning, to smoke and to cough early-morning phlegm into our tiny yard. He'd throw open the vertical blinds, slide open the shitty creaking glass patio door two feet from my head, not even trying to be quiet. In winter months it was the cold that woke me up first. The rest of the time, the noise.

During the summer, Shane's first objective in the morning was to turn off the air conditioning, which the landlord paid for. We kept it at a steady fifty degrees — perfect for going to bed, freezing to wake up to. The air conditioner, a window unit, was lodged directly above my fifty-dollar mattress. To turn it off, Shane used a broom, but not one of those plastic dollar-store brooms. This one was solid wood. When he reached too far and missed the dial, I was woken up by a broomstick to the face.

Shane and I were insanely competitive. Neither one of us had jobs but we'd bet fifty dollars on which character said "California" in the opening credits to *Real World 2* (it was Dominic). We scared people with our bets. Fifty or a hundred dollars to settle the most inane disputes. Who managed the New York Dolls? Was "tea" a slang word for marijuana in the Fifties (I was reading *On the Road*)? Is the word *license* spelled differently in British English? We always paid up, no matter the cost, but it put a real strain on our friendship. It was Shane's name on the lease, and as he constantly reminded me, he could kick me out at any time.

He stole my answering machine. I tried to stiff him on the rent in the summer. By the end of the one-year lease, we hated each other. After I moved out, Shane moved into the apartment across the hall, where he said it was easier to maneuver his wheelchair. I came over to help him set up his bed, and since that visit we've rarely seen each other. Visiting his new place was always weird — it looked exactly like my old apartment, but in reverse. The carpet was green now and the door was on the side of the kitchen instead of the living room. That's how I started to approach our interaction, like it was false, a backwards mirror image of how we used to talk to each other.

Today Shane is teaching Spanish at IU Southwest, the University of Louisville, and Jefferson Community College, and flipping me off from his car. "Hey you fuckin prick!" He locks my fingers under his, bent at the knuckles — the only way Shane ever shakes hands.

I tell him about my trip to Spain last year and my out-of-practice Spanish. When a man on the street asked for a light I told him "No fumar," which means "No smoking," and Danielle shrugged and added "No tienes fumar" — "You don't have to smoke."

Students rush past. Someone calls me Professor Hess and when they're out of earshot, we laugh like we're pulling something over on them. "So what have you been up to?" I ask. It's cold out here, and I'm late for my 2:30 class.

"Teaching, not much else. I've been really sick lately. My mom's staying with me for a few weeks... I don't know, not much else really." He breathes hard, looks at his floorboard. "What about you and Danielle?" Still married? Do we have kids? "Fuck, I don't know," he says. "I haven't talked to you in so long." He says he can't sleep at night, that he showed up to teach Spanish in his pajamas one morning last week, realized before he got out of the car at least, and had to call in to cancel class from a payphone across the highway. I laugh, and that makes him laugh too, but I don't think he told the story to be funny. We pause for a moment and study each other. He does look really pale.

"Well I better go teach."

"Yeah, I gotta get over to JCC. *Call* me — same number, same apartment."

Seventeen

I don't know if it's celebrating Halloween in June or what, but something has wrecked my sense of seasons, my perception of how time progresses. I've been an ice cream man and a stand-up comic. I've taken Icelandic poets to a Kentucky crud rock show, sold Billy Graham corndogs, and tortured people in a haunted morgue. And now, when it's time to choose this year's costume, I can't decide what I want to be.

The real Halloween comes mid-week, which gives people an excuse to throw parties both the weekend before Halloween and the weekend after. Danielle and I are invited to three parties, which we decide calls for three different costumes. She's an ice princess, a black fairy, a ballerina. I'm an undead trucker, then a ghost pimp, then, with my last remaining tube of face paint (yellow), a jaundice patient. The pimp and the patient are variations of old costumes, nothing I haven't done before. For the undead trucker, I use a trick my dad taught me. You can make believable tire tracks by spray-painting a tire and then pressing a t-shirt onto the wet paint. To add to the run-over effect, I rough up my face with some Zombie Flesh and swipe liquid latex and fake blood over that. Danielle's black fairy is a slight but distinct variation of her costume from June.

I'm trying to understand this tension I feel about how I spend my time and where I see all of it going. My friends feel it too, like we're all in a state of transition, all of us spending our time working toward something when we're not even sure we want what that something is. All the preparation that goes into becoming a professor or a doctor or a librarian, and the whole time you're asking yourself if that's what you really want to become. It's an easy cycle to get trapped in, and a hard one to drag yourself out of. The more you think about what you'll be doing in the future, the faster time seems to move. It gets tiring, but so does distracting yourself.

Chad and David have just finished a battery of med school exams, so a Halloween party sounds like a good place to relax. Although Chad may have taken it too far. Ten minutes after arriving, he's sprawled out facedown in the living room. Hasn't had one drink. He's just tired. All night people he's never met are stepping over him as they come in the door — "Who brought the cool kid?" We consider leaving him there, but we wake him up, and he goes home while we go to the next party.

✼ ✼ ✼

David takes Danielle and me to a Halloween party with his girl-friend Kitty and his gay friend James. He describes it as a "gay Halloween party," as if Gay Halloween is a different holiday entirely.

"Do you feel weird going to a gay party?" he asks me.

"No. Do you?"

"No. I mean, well kind of. But you know, James asked me and I'm going because I'm his friend… honestly though, it's not the people I'm most comfortable around."

For someone who's nervous around homosexuals, David makes the odd choice to dress up as a cowboy. He's just back from vacation at his family's ranch in Texas and he's been wearing a cowboy hat ever since, says he has to wear it consistently to break it in. Tonight he goes all out — tight jeans, chaps, a bandana, the works. James takes one look at Cowboy David and tells him his costume will be a real crowd-pleaser, which is good, because being the center of attention seems to make David relax. He's the belle of the ball.

The party is at the house of someone I don't know, a friend of David's friend, on an upscale street in the Highlands. James makes introductions at the door, calling me a comedian since that's what I was doing when I met him last month. I see one of my old professors, dressed up as a nun and surrounded by altar boys, ogle David as we make our way through the living room. The house is completely packed. Danielle and I squeeze past red body-painted devils and buxom drag queens, slowly making our way to the back deck for some beer. "Bud Lite or Natural Light?" she asks me.

"What?"

"It's all they have left."

"Dammit."

Men flood into the back room behind David. He demonstrates his lasso techniques and talks about his adventures at the ranch. He's loving the attention, can't stop grinning the entire time, flirting with the shirtless pirates and sailors that gather around him. Every few minutes we hear him say "No. I'm not gay. That's my girlfriend over there." He points, Kitty does sort of a half-hearted wave, and he goes back to entertaining. "No, I've never even tried it before."

Kitty sort of groans to Danielle, "I've never felt so unattractive."

Suddenly David's frowning and ready to go, and we head out the door and into the car, on to another party near Cherokee Park. Danielle and Kitty want to dance and James heads off in search of a restroom, which leaves me and a quiet, pensive David on a bench in the kitchen. "The costumes are better here," I say to David, "But nobody seems as friendly."

David's frown becomes more intense and he says, "That might not be such a bad thing." That's all he says, so I don't say anything else either. We watch Afro-Hippy play pool versus Colonel Sanders on Mini-stilts. We drink on the balcony. We wait in line for the bathroom. The five of us reunite in the kitchen — first David and I wander in there, then James, then Danielle and Kitty. We sit at the table and watch things wind down. We watch someone's dog sniff along the floor, drinking spilled beer and nibbling crumbs of Doritos and cigarette butts. Some people want to open the last bottle of wine, and they ask me if I think they should. When Raggedy Ann tries to open the refrigerator, she slips and falls on the tile. It happens again less than five minutes later. Raggedy Ann is still rubbing her ass when a different girl — a ballerina or cheerleader, something — hits the floor in the exact same spot.

David's had enough. He stands up, still in full cowboy gear, and walks over looking determined, looking like a true American hero. Is he going to towel off the floor? Comfort the princess? Draw up a "Caution" sign?

He rubs his boot back and forth across the spot. "It's slick," he announces.

It isn't until we're back in the car that David will explain why he left the Gay Halloween party in such a rush, and even then he explains it in his clinical doctor language. "One of those guys put his thumb on my anus."

Leaving early hadn't made any difference to me and Danielle. We were just floating from party to party, changing costumes along the way. I say floating because that weekend I felt like I was passing over it all, watching but not involved. In the car, Danielle asked me "Are you ok?"

I was ok, but I was quiet, like David was the last half of the night. Nobody touched my anus, but I was thinking about some things.

❀ ❀ ❀

I was thinking about how celebrating Halloween in June is like reclaiming time. We won't let them stop us. We won't let them tell us when Halloween is. Instead of following dates on a calendar, we took matters into our own hands and decided that October was too far away. Are there other things we could apply this to? Could I transport myself back in time by showing up at Shane's apartment across the hall from the old apartment I shared with him? Would that recapture that first year of college when everything I encountered seemed so new and Shane took me shoplifting and I sneaked into bars with him using his old I.D.? Or would that just be me visiting Shane, two lecturers trying to forget whatever caused them to stop speaking to each other in the first place? I think about it, but instead of visiting Shane, I go to another Halloween party at Jake and Carrie's house.

The ghost pimp walks up the front steps of an Eastern Parkway apartment building with no shirt, in Salvation Army red slacks with flat front and boot flare. He drapes Danielle's fuzzy winter coat over his shoulders and tops off the outfit with two final touches — a white-and-black striped nightcap, and a pair of toy boxing gloves that make a sound like glass breaking if you hit something or someone hard enough, and in just the right spot on the glove.

I'm a pimped-out, boxing ghost. Inside I remove the coat and gloves and my costume switches to Larry, the downstairs neighbor from *Three's Company*. I stand around combing my chest hair in imitation of one obscure running gag from that show. Danielle sports a black cape and heavy black eye makeup. Her original plan was to go this weekend as a Bastard Child, complete with diaper, pacifier and dirty t-shirt, but she changed her mind at the last minute. Jake opens the door as the Two of Diamonds, counterpart to Carrie's Alice. Lara wears a Cub Scout uniform. Will dresses up as his own uncle.

Carrie announces her new job ...as a *librarian*! I'm happy for her. This was her dream. I remember her last job seemed to take so much out of her. Even though she's excited, though, there's some dread in her voice. She and Danielle talk about how the worst thing about a job can be going in for your shift that first morning knowing that the rest of the mornings will pretty much be just like that one.

One of the best things about my own job is that the scenery

changes. I worried about sitting at the same desk and walking into the same classrooms every semester, but every semester the students are different. By the time I get tired of them, they move on to new classes and I get a new group of people. And if I teach the classes the same way, that's my fault. But at the same time I spend all day looking at writing and talking about writing. Then at night I'm writing myself. Danielle says a job can consume your enthusiasm for pretty much anything, and I worry about that happening.

It's hot in Jake and Carrie's apartment, so we huddle in the kitchen around the window unit air conditioner. Lara goes home early and Will and I eventually trade our original costumes for various skirts and dresses from Carrie's closet. We discover there's a bully lurking in Will. He's amazed by my sound-making boxing gloves, tries to buy them from me. He wants to turn our joking boxing match into a full-on brawl. "Hit me as hard as you can," he begs us. "Fuck it. I don't care anymore." And he doesn't. We have no fear now — Will has broken a barrier along with Nanine's toilet. Jake wants to box naked. Carrie flirts with Danielle. "You have the most beautiful ankles I've ever seen on a woman."

Will and Danielle get on the computer to update their Livejournals, rushing to document this night while it's still going on, before it has even fully happened, as if it's slipping away from them. They miss Carrie's dancing spree in the living room. She dances for hours. Jake and I shout names of music videos from our childhoods and she jumps into each one's choreography without pausing. Bell Biv Devoe, MC Serch, Kriss Kross — she remembers them all.

The whole night is on tape — hours of Halloween footage that came out silent because Jake forgot to turn on the microphone. Carrie was obsessed with videotaping. Earlier today she re-watched tapes of us from years ago. Tonight she set up the camera so that we could watch ourselves on the TV screen, watch it all as it happened. Danielle sent me to Winn-Dixie to buy snapshot film because she felt too weird going inside in her costume. And of course I'll go home and write stories about it. All of us, it's like we have a sense that tonight is something important, that we've captured something here.

❖ ❖ ❖

Our interest in documenting this year's Halloween leads me to question how long can this kind of stuff last before you're doing it just because you used to do it and you don't want to let it go? I'm feeling disconnected from the things I used to enjoy doing, and that's making me tired of my friends. I haven't had a lot of long-term friendships in my life, but the ones I did have, ended. True, I've known Chad since I was twelve, but we see each other so rarely that we've become more like acquaintances. There's been a point in most of my friendships where I got tired of my friends and I wanted out. I did it with Shane. I just stopped returning his phone calls. Now when I see him at work I feel guilty, which makes me want to avoid him, which makes me feel even guiltier. I tell Jake and Carrie how I ended my friendship with Shane and they tell me I'll do it to them someday too.

When they say it, I'm thinking no way, it'll never happen, but my friendship with them almost ended four years ago over a Beastie Boys show in St. Louis. My car was dying and in exchange for a four-hour ride, I paid for both their overpriced tickets. Carrie hated the show. Jake wanted me to pay all the gas money too, even though he used the trip as an opportunity to visit his family, who live exactly halfway to St. Louis. Things deteriorated over the weekend, and all of us came away feeling like we'd been ripped off in the deal. At the time I thought fuck it, it was worth it, and we didn't go to shows with them for a long time. We both got over it soon enough, but there for a moment Danielle and I would have traded one night with the Beastie Boys for five years with Carrie and Jake.

As people get older they don't tend to have as many friends or to make as many new ones. I don't know if that's because they replace friendships with work, or with time spent frustrated and hating work or watching TV to try to forget about work, but looking at the people I know it seems to be true. And when they do get together with friends, a lot of that time is spent complaining about work. That's why it starts to be easier to make friends with your co-workers instead of other people — everyone has to deal with assholes at work, but you can complain about the same assholes.

So recently I've made it a goal to bring the two worlds together. Adam is coming with Danielle and me to the Midwest Modern Languages Association Convention, and I asked Carrie to co-write a paper on hip-hop:

Day One: We spend two hours in the library at the University of Louisville's School of Music. Back issues of The Source and academic treatises on hip hop and identity theory (*See? I told you this stuff was fun*, I say to Carrie). At my apartment while Jake and Danielle are at work, we take notes from our sources and send off our proposal, a vague description of what the paper will eventually say. We're going somewhere with this. Everyone who has looked at hip hop before has been taking the wrong approach. We have the key. We're going to really work hard on this. Jake calls twice between calls from Danielle. Are they nervous about us spending so much time together, or just jealous we're not at work?

Day Two: We receive an e-mail response that our proposal has been accepted. Seeing that as enough progress for now, we spend the day drinking chocolate malts and watching zombie movies.

Day Three: Carrie quits, says she never thought it was such a good idea in the first place.

The paper is about rappers who wear masks: Humpty Hump, who ingeniously hit it big wearing a big-nose mask and writing songs against plastic surgery, and MF DOOM, who had an earlier record deal as a different rapper with a different name and is now back, in mask, as DOOM, vowing to seek his revenge on the record industry. Carrie is no longer interested, and Danielle and Jake are at work, so I sit alone in my living room, listening to DOOM's songs about how all his friends turned their backs on him. Thinking about masks and identity and perceptions, trying to reconcile who I was with who I'm becoming.

Eighteen

The lobby of the Cleveland Renaissance is giant and fancy. I come in wearing a frayed toboggan, carrying books and my clothes in a ratty cardboard box. This weekend is the annual Convention of the Midwest Modern Language Association. I'm tired. Not from driving but from everything — midterm grades, the Halloween season, an injured iguana, even running into Nichole and Shane, two people I thought I'd never see again. I don't want to go to the conference. I want to sleep. And then I decide I don't even want to do that — I just want to hide. I'm supposed to officially sign in at the conference this afternoon but I don't. We throw our stuff in the room and head out to the Flats.

Adam and Danielle have come along for the ride, to support me in my first year as chair of literary criticism, which sounds more impressive than it is — I raised my hand last year and nobody else wanted to do it. My job is to design a topic for the session, send out a call to professors and grad students whose research fits with that topic, then select the three best papers and invite their authors to read them out loud to an ever-shrinking audience. For this, I, and they, get a free trip to Cleveland. One of them has already cancelled.

Tonight it's quiet and artificially lit outside. The tops of the buildings look like Christmas lights and the streets are one long fluorescent corridor. The Flats is the old warehouse district and the new entertainment district. Chain restaurants and clubs have sprung up between rusted remnants of old steel bridges, ghosts from the industrial past. We see massive steel constructions now equipped with permanent lighting which casts a warm glow over Lake Erie. But something still looks evil about them. They rise threateningly over us. I hold Danielle's hand.

In the Flats we listen to a cover band — two guys on piano and keyboard — they ask for requests. Adam shouts out *Cat Stevens!* and when they start playing he mutters to Danielle, "This is the *last* Cat Stevens song I wanted to hear." They play Chuck Berry's "My Ding-aling," Jimmy Buffet, Billy Joel. They play "The Piano Man" twice. The guy on piano gets so excited during the keyboard solos that he plays percussion, furiously slamming the lid of his piano open and shut.

Adam is intent on discovering something new here in Cleveland, something unforeseen and mind-blowing, something we couldn't have expected. Adam approaches most things in his life this way. It's always endearing, but sometimes infuriating. It makes him more outgoing than I am. Outside the piano bar he spots three punk kids and approaches them to ask about good places to see shows or buy records. Adam trusts them to know these things because of dyed-black hair and the band patches sewn onto their jeans — always a risky equation. They could have had both done at the mall. They're high school juniors, we find out, and they make a consistent effort to make sure we know they have a band. "Yeah, our band's practice space is a cool place to hang out. That's basically all we do — just hang out there and play music."

"And write songs."

"Yeah, and write songs for our *band*."

They've never met anyone from Kentucky. "Is that where they fry all the chicken?" They approach their neighboring state as if it lies across a vast ocean, as if our journey has taken us months. "Wow, what are you doing here?"

Adam is fielding the questions. "Mickey's here for work — MLA convention." Could have been a good name for their band.

"Well I hope you didn't come up here thinking Cleveland's exciting." We had.

When I first told Adam I was coming to this conference, he said "Cleveland!" like a game show announcer — "Acapulco!" But this was northern Ohio, in November.

"Can Danielle go with you?"

"Yeah. She always goes with me to conferences. Do you know we haven't spent one night apart in six years?"

"Oh that's right. How was your anniversary?"

"Two months ago?"

"Really? It hasn't been that long, has it?" I could see him adding the weeks in his head. Adam will do this. He will sit and process a piece of information — something like the date of your own anniversary, something you should know — until he can prove to himself that you're right. "Wow, I guess I should give you guys your present."

For our sixth wedding anniversary, Adam has bought us two free passes to laser tag. But we can't have them yet. He has a second pair of passes, and he's holding all four until he finds a fourth person, a girl, who wants to come with us, like a double date. "That way I get to see you use your present!" It will be almost a year before he sullenly hands me all four tickets, which then double as a gift for our seventh wedding anniversary.

"Man, Cleveland!"

"Yeah. You wanna come with us?"

"Yeah! I mean, well, I don't want to mess up your and Danielle's romantic getaway." It's an academic conference. It's Cleveland.

Also, this may be one of our last chances to hang out with Adam. He's moving soon. He's going to Chicago as phase one of his plan to establish himself as a full-time comedian. We can go visit him — it's only a five-hour drive — but I'll miss having him right down the street. I'll miss the excitement he has for everything.

The three of us wander through the streets, led by Adam, who now is determined to find the Cleveland Improv. He knows a comedian there, but not well enough, as it turns out, to get us in free. He talks comedy in the Improv bar while Danielle and I play air hockey and skeeball in the late-night arcade next door. We win tickets and trade them for Jolly Ranchers and grape Now N Laters. The Basketball Supershoot is out of order.

It's not that we're not having fun, but we had expected more. From the other of side the bridge, from outside our hotel, this part of town had looked so alluring, but down here in the middle of it, there's nothing to see.

❋ ❋ ❋

The highlights of this year's conference program include sessions on academic celebrity, on the exploitation of part-time lecturers. There's a paper about Dolly Parton, a session on *South Park* and *The Simpsons*. There's "The Literature of Amplification: Third Wave Feminist Consciousness-Raising at the Rock and Roll Crossroads," and "Re-reading Dick and Jane: Interrogating Whiteness in the Freshman Composition Classroom." But I can't concentrate right now.

I want to explain it to Adam and Danielle, this stagnation I feel, this feeling that everything I've ever been involved in amounts to "nothing much." It sounds awful to put into words, though, so I don't do it. I settle for these scattered pieces of conversation that never really seem to meet or connect. Adam tests out new jokes or paper ideas, Danielle talks nonstop about cave paintings, about ghost pictures she saw on the Internet. And it seems like we're listening. We nod and ask questions to prompt the rest of the story. But we're like Latin professors at a Norse Mythology session — we're not quite paying attention.

This afternoon I skip part of the conference to see Henry Rollins speak at Case Western Reserve University. Rollins wrote the book — not a metaphor, but an actual book — on punk touring. *Get in the Van: On the Road with Black Flag.* He runs a small publishing company, 2.13.61, named for his birthday. For me, Rollins is a punk turned writer, for Adam he's a punk comedian. Rollins has done spoken word tours for years now, but only recently has he started to call himself a comic rather than a speaker or storyteller. Adam's excited. We arrive at Case Western two hours early to make sure we get tickets.

During our wait, Adam bugs me with questions about his paper for W290, Writing in the Arts & Sciences. He wants to write about *Jim's Journals*, a comic strip that ran a few years ago in college newspapers. "My idea is to focus on the character of Tony…" Tony is Jim's roommate in the comics. Adam's theory is that Tony is a pitiable character, that although he's really negative and abrasive, deep down he's sensitive and alone. "He's always getting excited about something new, like clipping grocery coupons or lifting weights or drinking eight glasses of water a day. But he always gives up on them so quickly. It's like he's searching so hard for something he can identify himself with." Adam is still in the pre-writing stages and he bombards me with questions — not even questions, really, like he's sitting there brainstorming out loud and not even writing any of it down. That's what I keep saying — "yeah, write that down!" And finally he gets out his notebook and can't remember anything he said.

He gives up working on his paper and asks Danielle and me if we want to hear about his new idea to make money writing greeting cards. "A lot of comedians have these side jobs to support their career onstage, so I was thinking I could do like funny birthday cards or Get Well Soon cards or something …what do you guys think about this one — *Happy 30th Wedding Anniversary Mom and Dad. I'm flaming gay!*"

"Or *Sorry you lost a foot,*" Danielle adds.

"How about *Happy Birthday, you blind motherfucker?*"

More people crowd into the foyer of the auditorium and Danielle and I eavesdrop on a conversation behind us, between three Case Western art students excited to see Henry Rollins:

"We might hang out and try to meet him afterward."

"Not me. I'm staying at Kristy's so I'm out of here." This guy checks his cell phone messages while he talks to his friends. "Plus, I'm not really into shaking hands with people. I mean, if I could really *hang out* with someone maybe, but not just introduce myself. Because he doesn't know who I am."

"Yeah. Maybe if we brought him some cookies or something."

·"I have cookies in my car."

"Yeah!"

"We can't take your cookies."

Rollins does comedy mixed with political messages for probably an hour and a half. He talks about the differences between men and women. He talks against reactionary patriotism and tells a joke about sweating. Right on cue, as soon as he launches into the set-up, we can tell his gray t-shirt is no match for the heat of the spotlights. Sweat springs up immediately and it never really spreads. The same places get sweatier and sweatier, forming a strange pattern on the front of his shirt. Danielle points it out as we're leaving. "Didn't that sweat stain look like a monkey's face?" Adam had seen it too.

So I forfeit a few conference hours of Cervantes and Milton to hear the living, breathing word of Henry Rollins. The next day, we pass up the Rock and Roll Hall of Fame for real, live rock and roll at a dive bar.

The Puta-pons are two young women with dark lipstick and tight skirts, and a male drummer who looks like he'd be into science. Adam has defined their central dilemma — "Sucks to be a hot girl in a band. You're up there playing your heart out and everyone's thinking about your boobs!"

Danielle wants a bag of tortilla chips from the bar and I scour the list of ingredients before I pay. Adam cites his new don't ask, don't tell version of vegetarianism. "If a chicken's in there, I don't want to know about it." Two years ago Adam was completely vegan. I went vegetarian myself because of Decimus and a series of nightmares about people trying to eat her. First it was Jake, then our cats, then Bragi and Michael, and then in the most horrific dream I was chasing her around with a fork. It's tough to have a friend so low on the food chain.

I buy Adam a beer and we watch the show with our elbows propped on the bar. If this is the last time I'm going to hang out with him I want it to feel like it. And standing here and not saying anything feels like an ending to me. The Puta-pons end their set and make way for Enon — Danielle's reason for bringing us to the Grog Shop tonight. Enon has risen from the ashes of Brainiac, a great Dayton band whose singer died in a car crash in 1997. Same guitarist, but Enon is clearly its own band. Tonight they play loud and hard. Adam stuffs toilet paper into his ears.

❊ ❊ ❊

With Adam moving soon I'm thinking about concentrating more on my friends. I feel like Danielle and I are losing touch with Jake and Carrie, who have been our best friends for so long. But more than that I'm thinking about Shane and how I turned my back on him for basically being himself, how all the things that pissed me off about him have turned into funny stories that make me miss him when I tell them to people. Shane was never easy to get along with. His closest friends tended to shake their heads or grimace when I told them I was planning on becoming his roommate. But he's very good at apologizing, which is something I've never been good at. I tend to just stop returning his calls to avoid the confrontation.

I'm thinking I should give him a call and apologize. I even think about borrowing Adam's cell phone in the bar and calling from there, but I don't. Then it's so weird — when I check email back at the hotel, there's a message from the Spanish department at IU Southwest asking if I've heard from him this week. I picture him rolling around campus in his pajamas, hiding from his superiors, but then I remember how pale he looked when I saw him and how I'd never heard him complain about being sick the way he did then — when I lived with him, he refused to show any signs of weakness. I still have his phone number, my old number, memorized, so I call, but I just get his voicemail.

❊ ❊ ❊

I walk past conference participants all weekend, see them with their clip-on laminated nametags. It's the kind of thing I appreciate at most out-of-town conferences, something that says "Hey — that guy's one of us." We can spot each other across parking lots, give the MLA thumbs up. But in Cleveland I leave mine in the hotel room. I walk around for three days in the same clothes and then at the last minute before my session, I ask Adam and Danielle to pick out my most academic-looking sweater to offset the fact that I haven't shaved or taken a shower since the day before we left Louisville. Now I'll look more intense than sloppy. I pin on the nametag.

Nobody comes to my session — not even presenters. Out of the three speakers I selected; only one, Pat Bizarro, shows up. It's me, Pat, and a woman named Audrey who has to leave early. Is this some kind of conference karma? Are people completely uninterested in our topic of Interpretation in the Writing Classroom? We wait fifteen minutes, because maybe they're just late. Soon, though, it's absolutely clear no one is coming. We pull our chairs into a tiny circle and Pat reads us part of his paper. He talks about how to comment on writing without taking over the paper — how to return the authority to the student. He applies Wolfgang Iser's theory of indeterminacy to the teaching of creative writing. He proposes that the implied reader is constructed by the words on the page. Then Audrey has to go.

And so ends our ill-fated session. Pat and I stand around for a few minutes, drinking lukewarm MMLA water from sad little styrofoam cups. We talk about professional kinds of things like how nobody seems to come to these late afternoon sessions. He asks me what kind of an English program we have at IUS and I say a pretty good one. I ask him if he's ever worked with a professor I know there, and he says he has. We stand there in our assigned room almost as long as the session itself had been scheduled to last. Is it out of some sense of obligation, or just not knowing what to do with ourselves, seeming so useless here in the empty conference room. Finally, though, we walk out together and there are Danielle and Adam waiting, sitting in the floor in the hallway. Adam jumps up and asks if I think he can run down the stairs fast enough to beat the elevator. "Let's race!" he says.

Waiting for Adam down in the lobby, Danielle and I pick up a free guide to Cleveland entertainment. We see that Pharcyde and Souls of Mischief are playing here two days after we leave. *Dammit*. This is the third time I've narrowly missed seeing the Pharcyde play. It's like I'm cursed. But this time I don't let it get to me. I know it would have been a weak, straggling version of the Pharcyde anyway — only two members are left of the original four. This realization fits perfectly into the feel of this weekend, my Cleveland feeling — strangely content and defeatist at the same time. Like it could have been good, was almost *really* good, but then it wasn't.

Man, it could've been great. I was sincerely looking forward to the opportunity to stand at a podium and introduce someone named Dr. Bizarro. I'm sure Pat hears it all the time, but Danielle and I had spent weeks laughing at the idea that he might turn out to be an evil, cartoonish villain. He wouldn't even have a presentation. He'd just stand in front of the audience wringing his hands and laughing maniacally — Dr. Bizarro with his Grammar Ray.

Nineteen

While I was in Cleveland, Shane died in a hospital in Louisville. Shane — we used to get so pissed off at each other that he'd want to turn it into an actual fistfight. Once we were trapped inside the apartment together during a blizzard. We put balled-up socks over our hands and to level the playing field we fought on our elbows in the floor of our shitty apartment.

Shane taught me to drive on the Interstate. He washed my clothes after he introduced me to vodka and orange juice and I claimed I could drink more than anybody — "It doesn't affect me!" I dragged him backwards up stairs when he wanted to talk to that girl on the third floor, and picked him up off the floor when he laughed so hard that his chair tipped over.

He told people I was his embarrassingly uncool younger brother. If Shane and I actually had been brothers, though, we would have had something to force us to talk to each other. We hadn't spoken in two years, really. We were over the apartment stuff but had lost contact and lost interest. Six months after I moved out, Shane called me to apologize. I apologized too, and we ate burritos. We spent some time together in the months after that — late night trips to Wal-mart, hurried fake announcements over an unmanned PA station in housewares. But it all ended soon enough. Shane could make me hate him like no one else and then apologize so sincerely that I had to question if it was sincere, because nobody could be *that* sincere, could they? And so eventually I was finished with it. Shane and I could never get along for an extended period of time, and this was early into my relationship with Danielle. I had found the one person I truly wanted to spend my time with, and everyone else was peripheral.

I didn't have much patience for Shane, and he was going through a weird stage at the same time, sort of purposefully alienating everyone. I saw it and I complained about it at home with Danielle. I never pointed it out to him the way he would have done with me. Directness was Shane's primary characteristic. He'd say things:

"That shirt makes you look like a pussy,"

"You *sold* me this shirt."

"Yeah, well that's why I sold it. Besides, it didn't look pussy on me."

But he would also admit how much he envied some quality of yours. He never held back, and when he lied he was honest about it later.

They hold his memorial at Jefferson Community College. Everybody calls him Jeff at the service. That was his professional name. After the service, people eat bland sugar cookies and don't know what to say to each other. Doug is here, and Dean. Shane's brother Ryan. People Danielle and I haven't seen in years, who have driven from out of town. Our old mutual roommate Chris is here — balder, but with longer hair. We all get a little card with his picture and an inscription that says how much he loved teaching.

And he loved JCC. Shane used to have a framed picture of the main building in his apartment. He had taken it at night with his professional camera and I thought it was some European castle. I had noticed the architecture before, but Shane's version looked so much more magnificent. Goddammit, we worked at this same school, in this same building, and really never made an effort to talk to each other. We were over the whole apartment situation — who wronged who didn't matter anymore, but the whole thing had disintegrated into disinterest. I was still excited to see him when it happened by accident, but I never made a point to keep in contact. I still told stories about him, how he gave my Nirvana book to some friend of his in the army, just because he knew I hated the guy, just to be a dick. Then two years later he bought me a Frank Zappa book and said we were even. It's like all of my Shane stories start out with him being an asshole. When I tell people about him, I can see it in their reactions. But in the end they can't help laughing, wishing they knew this guy. Shane was always entertaining but so hard to take when he didn't laugh, or when you couldn't laugh with him. That's where we hit walls with each other. That day at IUS. Three weeks ago he sounded so sincere telling me "Something's wrong with me, seriously," but Shane was sincere about everything, and he didn't sound scared that day.

Dead at thirty-three. Same age as the Human Beatbox. People ask me what killed him and I don't know. I don't want to know. All I can say is he was sick and he didn't have health insurance. He had teaching awards but no medical benefits.

The last time I saw Shane he was this mysterious figure, face blocked by a sun visor, flipping me off from the driver's seat of his car. I still told stories about Shane, but I had no idea about new details from his life. He told me that day that he was sick, and I see now that he was. He looked pale, yellow, and his voice was weak. Shane had never taken care of himself. "Fuck, Mick. I don't know what's wrong with me."

"Have you gone to the doctor?"

"No. Hnnngghh" — one of those Shane snort-laughs.

And that was the last thing I said to him — "Go to the doctor."

✿ ✿ ✿

Let me admit something. I have typed my own name into Internet search engines to see what comes up.

Let me admit something else. I have done this more than once.

At that Beastie Boys show in St. Louis they wouldn't let Danielle in with her chain wallet and I didn't speak up when they told her to throw it away at the door. Let me make clear that I love the Beastie Boys, and that Tribe Called Quest was opening and I had waited my entire youth and driven four hours to see this show. So when the wallet hit the garbage can and I should have stood up for her, I was like fuck it. Forget it. Let's get to our seats.

I know it was just an object, just a little piece of fake leather she attached to her hip with a chain the guards claimed could be used as a weapon. But Danielle loved that wallet, to a degree I only realized after she lost it.

I was late to Shane's memorial service.

Once when Shane said something I knew was wrong, I looked it up and then casually mentioned the fact two days later. When he disagreed with me, I challenged him to a bet, knowing I wouldn't lose. I admitted this to him later, but I refused to give back his 25 dollars (Shane would have done the same thing -- he tried to hire one of his friends to call me and pretend to be an MTV producer to settle our Real World bet).

I got a D in Beginning Guitar. I stopped going to class, and I refused to take the final. I'm a horrible example.

Each of my parents has called me at separate times to apologize for things about my childhood. I had no idea what to say to either of them.

Some mornings when I was teaching too many classes, I'd forget to feed Decimus and leave her hungry til I got home, or forget to turn off her Vita-light when it got dark outside, leaving the poor diurnal creature awake, believing this must be the longest day ever.

I used to scream at my parents for not having more money. I used to correct my mom's grammar. I smashed a hole in her bedroom door and it's still there today.

I don't visit my grandmother as much as I should.

I don't massage Danielle as much as I should, unless I think it will lead to sex.

And I didn't call Shane. I told him I would that day but I never intended to, really. The idea left my head as soon as I made the promise. I'm sorry. I'm sorry I didn't come to your party that night two years ago with your international students. You were teaching English as a second language and called me up at the last minute to hang out at your tiny apartment with people from Bosnia and Botswana. You were teaching them to curse in English, which I know was the secret joy you took in the job.

I had plans already that night, but I could have broken them, or ended them early. I thought about student events I'd planned myself, the impossibility of it all. I worried that no one was actually coming to your party, and I still didn't go. I walked around looking at Christmas lights with my friends, drinking free hot chocolate from the cookie place, and I thought of you alone in your apartment, smoking and staring out your vertical blinds into the snow.

Spring Semester

Twenty

It's hard to believe now that I didn't see any significance to the fact that he told me he could walk in his dreams, that the wheelchair never made an appearance. To the fact that he would stop his car, unload his chair, and set up his tripod on the side of the highway.

It's hard to believe that he kept pictures of me passed out drunk and naked and that as many people as he showed them to, I never found out until after he died.

That he laughed so hard I thought he was crying when he read the story I wrote about him for my freshman orientation class: "My biggest challenge in adapting to college life has been my roommate, who has an odd fascination with growing his facial hair to resemble Tex Watson or various other members of the Manson Family. He killed our house-plants on purpose. He makes me look at his genitals."

That even after he laughed that hard he said "It's funny, but it does-n't really have any depth." Which was what he said about everything I wrote.

That when he screamed "Oh shit, come in here and look at this!" I always looked, and it was always his dick, or photographs of his girl-friend naked so that later when we were eating at Taco Bell he could say "So Samantha, I caught Mickey looking at those pictures we took of you."

That still today, when people call for me to look at something, I expect that it will be somebody naked, or that I will be shown a photo of a dead raccoon, legs crushed behind him on the highway.

It was the raccoon that he showed me that day in his bedroom, the last day we lived in the apartment together, when his voice got quiet before he slid the picture back into the shoebox. "This is the one that made me stop taking pictures of road kill, but it's the only one I kept."

"You had a whole series of these?"

"Yeah. Don't you think that's fucked up? I mean, don't you think it's some kind of reflection on my motorcycle wreck?"

He was taking psychology classes and I was failing literary criticism. That year I believed nothing meant anything.

Twenty-one

When Chad calls, I tell him the bad news. He wasn't really that close to Shane anymore, but I can tell it hits him hard. All he asks is what happened. He doesn't say anything else and neither do I. Chad stares at cadavers all day and cuts people open and sees patients die on the operating table, but this is my first friend to die and as far as I know it might be Chad's first too. He's the only person I feel like I can talk to about it, but we don't really talk. Still, I feel more comfortable acknowledging it with him because he was there when I knew Shane, when I lived with him and Chad came over to see our apartment and we all drove to Action World to play arcade games. We changed a mall marquee to say "Old Dirty Panties — Two for $1" and Shane almost choked himself laughing. When something was funny, Shane thought it was funny on a different level than everyone else. He could laugh at something that I never would have considered funny, and I'd still crack up days later, just remembering him laughing about it.

So tonight I play pool with Chad and we don't talk about Shane. He invites me and Danielle to come with him to New Orleans this weekend. He has an interview at a hospital there, crossing his fingers to become a surgery resident. He's leaving in three months either way — if not New Orleans to some other city. So there's no way I can turn down the trip. Even beyond the goodbye aspect, I jump at the chance to get out of my apartment, to get away from Louisville and all those places that remind me that Shane is dead.

In New Orleans our jackets feel sweltering. Hours pass before our bodies have adjusted and it seems cold outside again. We're here for the first weekend of Mardi Gras parades. This morning we saw an older guy show his pecker and I watched an incredible scene with an impossibly cocky policeman who wouldn't step aside when the high school bands came through. Trumpeters sidestepped him all morning, baton twirlers had to dodge him to keep their rhythm. This cop was driving me insane — meandering here and there in the street with his dark-tinted cop sunglasses, with his hands folded behind his back like he's out for an afternoon stroll. Then — then the flag bearers come through from some inner city high school. And they're not *carrying* the flag, not like the other schools have been. These two kids each hold up an end of a huge sideways flagpole, and they swing it back and forth like a weapon, like a battering ram. Their band helmets are cocked to the side and they look like No Limit soldiers, walking at the front of their school's band not to lead the way but to clear it, to say *We're here, motherfucker*. The cop sees them coming — there's no way he doesn't see them — but he doesn't move. It's a point of pride for him now that all the bands break their marches to move around him, because wherever he's standing, that's *his* spot. And then the flag guys come through and plow their flagpole right into his chest. It almost knocks him over.

We're staying at a place Danielle found online, a B&B — Bed and Bar. Instead of a crappy toast-and-jelly breakfast, we get free drink tokens everyday. They're very generous — the housekeeper just tosses a random handful onto our table every morning. We count them into our stockpile of free stuff we've collected so far in New Orleans — matchbooks from the fancy cigar shop, beads caught mostly by Chad and Danielle at the parade, and the amazing plastic backscratcher that Danielle snatched off the ground for me as the last floats went by.

Our room is right above the bar, on the second floor of this corner building on Royal Street at the edge of the French Quarter. I'm outside writing on the balcony, and planning classes for next semester. I'm not writing about anything immediate — I'm writing plans for things, or rethinking things that have already happened. Danielle's inside reading Anne Rice. We're killing time waiting for Chad to get back from the hospital, waiting for a cab to pull up to the corner and for Chad to step out in his fancy interview suit he keeps in a long plastic bag. All he wears in the hotel room is his baggy white underwear. Danielle woke up this morning with his package staring her in the face. He was trying to shut off the alarm clock. While I'm waiting on the balcony, Chad calls our room from a payphone downstairs in the bar. Turns out he's been down there for over an hour.

Last night outside Jackson Square Chad paid a toothless woman to read his fortune, asked her what she sees for him and then told her his exact situation — "The reason I ask is because I'm moving soon, to another city to finish medical school. And I guess what I want to know is not so much where I'll be going, but will I be happy there? Will I make new friends? Will I still keep in touch with old ones …?"

The fortune teller nods, taking in Chad's preamble before she breaks out the tarot cards. "I see a move," she says.

Chad asks the fortune teller the question everyone wants to ask her. "Will I be happy?"

"Not at first."

Chad's destiny set, we collect today's free drink chips and prepare to head into the streets of the Quarter. We walk to St. Louis Cemetery even though we'd been warned by the woman at the tourist board not to go near there without a tour group — "It's next to the housing projects," she'd said. When we get there the place is so overrun with tourist groups that we can't even see what we want. One of them blocks the tomb of voodoo queen Marie Leveau, the one grave Danielle really wants to see, and we stand patiently, waiting for the barking tour guide to finish her speech so they can move on and we can get a look for ourselves.

She stops mid-sentence, though — clears her way through her tour group to tell us we can join the tour for $20 like everyone else. Otherwise we can leave. "This is a private tour and *you* are not part of it."

Chad and I take a few steps back to pretend to be interested in a totally random grave while we wait, but Danielle doesn't budge. I'm proud of her. She stays right where she is, looking straight ahead at Marie Leveau's tomb. The tour guide stops again to threaten her, but Danielle isn't moving.

"I'm just waiting for you to get out of my way."

The tour guide knows she's beaten, so she gives up, shakes a finger at us and leaves it at that — "What you're doing is *stealing*."

Stealing like charging people to visit a public graveyard? Stealing like selling tickets to somebody's final resting place?

Danielle uses an entire roll of film to document the decaying graves, but I'm ready to move on. Where did she develop this interest in graveyards anyway?

❖ ❖ ❖

Tonight we let Chad choose the bar. The band's playing "All Night Long" by the Commodores and Danielle declares it her new theme song. Is mine still "Smells Like Teen Spirit?" A sour-faced girl around our age is dancing on the bar. Chad buys fruity expensive drinks in souvenir glasses he doesn't keep. My back scratcher snaps in two when it catches someone's jacket on the way up the stairs. *Fuck*. It was the same as the ones Shane and I got as presents from his girlfriend and a girl I followed around for six months. They bought them for us as house-warming presents for our new apartment. That one got broken too. Plastic crap.

We get a seat in the outdoors part of the bar, the courtyard — we're right next to the giant glimmering fountain and underneath some sort of heat lamp, like Decimus' Repti-Lamp on a larger scale. Danielle is cold anyway. She's rubbing her arms as she waits in line for the rest-room, which starts two hundred feet from us, but ends not far from our table. Danielle turns and waves to us from her spot at the very back.

"All drunken silliness aside, you're really lucky to have such an attractive and fun wife as Danielle." This is how Chad talks. This is what he said.

And I said, "I know."

It was the first truly honest moment of the weekend, and I didn't know how to respond. We probably hadn't said ten sentences to each other since we drove to the airport in Louisville. I sat in the terminal reading *The Rise of the Network Society* and Chad and Danielle read vampire novels. Then yesterday Chad was preoccupied with his interview and when I walked through the Quarter with Danielle, my mind was on shitty teaching evaluations from last semester and how everything seems finished. Now Chad's being sincere and I have nothing to give him in return. I feel stuck, like I can't open my mouth and I'm afraid if I do it'll all come pouring out and I don't want to listen to myself. I know it's there, but I don't want to hear it.

Usually it's easy to talk to Chad, but here I can't talk to anyone. Conversations with him are so good because he's always sleepy so they all feel like those late night conversations you'd have with friends sleeping over. At night, in sleeping bags, rambling on about whatever comes into your head, things that seem so profound and entertaining.

Chad sits here assessing me through half-shut eyes. First meeting him, you might think he's really smug. But he's just tired. He asks if Danielle and I have thought about having kids and I turn the conversation to our pets. He wants to talk about people we used to know, people from high school, but especially our first year of college, that first year that we lived in Louisville but spent our time mostly with everyone else who had moved there from our hometown. Some of them went back home after one semester, some of them spent time in rehab. One of our friends showed up on Jerry Springer in a three-way relationship — she still lives in Kentucky somewhere, but nobody's heard from her. We're still in Louisville — me and Chad, Louisville students forever. But now he's leaving and I'm the only one left, just me and Danielle. David's moving to Birmingham. Adam's in Chicago. And Shane isn't anywhere, which is what Chad brings this all back around to:

"It's really sad that Shane's dead."

"I know."

Twenty-two

Semesters have their own personalities. This was Shane's theory, his advice to a young kid starting college. He made sense. Fall 1993 was full of promise — too much. In three days back to back we had the chance to see Nirvana play Dayton, Kurt Vonnegut read in Lexington, and Dead Milkmen play Cincinnati on Halloween. We missed the Dead Milkmen — something had to be sacrificed. The following spring, though, brought no concerts at all, except sad David Lee Roth playing the Toy Tiger across the road from our apartment, the same club he's playing this spring, seven years later. No more Dead Milkmen, no more Nirvana. But David Lee Roth, he's perennial.

Shane was college to me. He was that first year away from home and the freedom of not being forced into classrooms for six hours a day. He was fearless in every way that I was intimidated by things. I had grown up very overprotected, but within weeks he had me betting people how much vodka I could drink and using his old I.D. to get into clubs. Living across from the Toy Tiger was the perfect excuse to see bands that were far past their prime open for wet t-shirt contests and foxy boxing. The most excited I ever saw Shane get was when Bad Brains played there. We were right down in front. I always thought it was amazing how Shane would get down front at those shows. When we saw Nirvana, there was this raised platform, all the way in the back of the enormous hockey arena, and that was where everyone in a wheelchair was supposed to watch the show. But Shane, he was down by the stage.

At Bad Brains the bouncers had this chain they were using to keep people off the stage. They weren't hitting us with it or anything. They just stretched it across the stage and stood there making sure nobody tried to go under or over it. I guess they were trying to keep people from jumping onstage or whatever, but Shane kept unhooking the chain from the wall and throwing it down on the floor. The bouncers

193

would come over and re-attach it, but he finally ripped out the little hook they were latching it to.

He kept ordering 75-cent screwdrivers and slamming me into everybody. Once the music got going, he grabbed me by the belt loop and started throwing me into people right and left. I was getting the hell knocked out of me, but we were both having such a good time with it that I held on as long as I could. This was his way to mosh.

When the crowd settled down, Shane motioned me down to him and asked if I'd do him a favor. He needed to go to the bathroom, but the restrooms in the Toy Tiger are all so old and shitty that they're not really handicapped accessible. There was no way he could fit his chair in the stall.

His only other option was this big trough like at elementary schools. It looked like it was built for about twenty people. Shane had to use catheters, which was a pretty big operation I guess, so he didn't want to have ten guys on each side of him while he pissed. His idea was that we'd wait until it was empty, and then I'd stand outside and ask people not to go in 'til he was finished. I said ok.

I didn't understand, because Shane loved nothing more than showing people his dick. I swear he had a list somewhere, and he just crossed off everyone's name as he got to them. And he had all these creative ways to get you to look at it. Right in the middle of a pawn shop or wherever, he'd just unzip his pants and say "Hey! Check out what I found."

The music was getting louder. Bad Brains was rocking the main stage, and on the other side of the restrooms the homemade bikini show was really heating up. Shane peeked around to make sure the last guy had left the restroom, then he headed inside. I stood guard. I don't think it was thirty seconds before I had to stop the first guy.

It's not exactly the best position to be in, calling everyone over as they head in to piss. Especially on 75 cent night. I had to stop them all one by one and lean in real close to their ears. "Hey, my friend's in there, and he's in a wheelchair, so could you wait just a minute til he comes out?"

The first couple of guys were really calm about the whole thing. One of them said "I know how it is, buddy." Then more and more people started coming up faster. I was still able to stop them all, but I told the whole story to the 5th or 6th guy and he nodded his head and everything, then he just stumbled on inside.

Everyone else I had stopped followed him in. I guess they thought I'd been playing some strange prank.

I lived with Shane in these apartments called Sans Souci, which means either carefree or careless in French. ·

He liked to fall asleep with a lit cigarette in his mouth. Any piece of fabric in our apartment had at least one hole in it.

When he was in my car and I was driving, he'd punch me, out of nowhere, in the face.

"Mother*fuck*er." Rubbing my jaw, swerving back onto the highway. "Come on," Laughing. "Can't you take a punch?"

All this was balanced out by the fact that once every two weeks or so, more often in icy weather, Shane and his wheelchair would topple sideways off the crude wooden ramp that our Sans Souci landlord built for him, and I would pull him off the cold ground and lift him by his underarms, like an impossibly heavy four-year-old, back into his chair.

I remember he fell over once when we were crossing the intersection to buy another bottle of vodka. I guess he drank most of the first one. It was the night before we went to the Nirvana show, and we were both almost laughing too hard to get Shane back in his chair. The second time I dropped him he punched me, and I punched him back, hard. These old guys who run the liquor store were standing at the window just staring at us.

We'd bought tickets the morning they went on sale, but I didn't realize I needed to make a special request not to be seated. So I was stuck in the bleachers. When Nirvana came on there was this huge surge of people from the seats jumping the rails and running down to the floor. This guy sitting behind me was one of the first to go. He pretty much jumped right over me. I started to follow him, but something held me back for one second too long. By the time I let go of my chair, the floor was entirely full from all directions and there were security guards pushing people back into their seats.

That was five concerts before the last show Nirvana would ever play. Kurt Cobain would be dead in four months. Shane would be dead in a few years, and the rest of us too, eventually. In a way, I can appreciate how staying in my seat let me see the stage so much better than I could have from the back of the floor. But I think about Shane, and something still bothers me about watching it from the outside, not being right down there in the middle of things.

Twenty-three

Alkaholiks shows have a reputation for turning into riots — not violent, destructive riots, just this frenzy of energy and broken bottles ... and breasts, which is why Danielle stays home. As much as she loves the Alkaholiks, sometimes an energetic rap show just isn't the best place to be a woman.

This is the first out-of-town show I have ever gone to by myself, which makes it an entirely different experience. Carrie didn't want to come for the same reasons as Danielle, and Jake didn't want to come without Carrie. But I think about Shane down in front at that Nirvana show and me standing way back behind the railing, and I drive to Cincinnati.

The UC basketball game means no parking anywhere near Vine Street, so I leave my car in a depressing, run-down neighborhood six or seven blocks away. Some little kids yell threats at me. At the club a short line has formed. A bartender steps outside to tell us to stay single-file and to stay against the wall. Cops on horses threaten to give people citations for parking in the fire station lot next door. Two homeless people try to sell us deodorant.

I get there early enough to stake out my spot directly in front of the stage. Tonight is the Alkaholiks tenth anniversary show — that's ten years, not ten concerts. It makes me inevitably happy to know that in ten more years they'll probably still be out here. They aren't touring on the strength of a hit single, but just skill and energy and their own excitement. They spray beer on us — Heineken — not the cheap stuff. They pass a bottle of gin to the crowd. J-Ro reminds us that he grew up just down the road in Columbus, and shows off the O-H-I-O tattoo across his knuckles.

They play all the songs I came to hear — Only When I'm Drunk, 40 oz. Quartet, Hip Hop Drunkies. They make us wait for Last Call. Tash teases us with the opening throughout the show — "Hey bartender, lemme get a rum'n'coke" — and then they play something else. They're building up to it, saving it for the end. Their big-energy closer. It will finish the night off after the on-stage beer-drinking competition. But I can't hold my spot that long. I'm dressed for 20-degree weather and it's 120 in here. I give up and stumble to the bar sweaty but with dry lips, eyes glazed. I had been at the front of the stage since the opening act, and had felt the crowd swell and encroach on my spot as the more popular acts came on, but I wasn't moving. I was dedicated. I had earned my spot. Eventually I was so packed in I couldn't move my arms. When Tash said put your hands in the air, it was all I could do to squeeze one of them free.

By this point in the show, I'm the lone sober person in the crowd, abstaining for the long drive back to Louisville. Although if I do get pulled over I'm not going to make a very convincing argument — I look like a zombie and smell like the case after case of Heineken sprayed on the front rows. But I hold steady, trying to stay focused and awake for my trip. The bartender grudgingly pours me a Coke, then waves me off like it's not even worth his trouble to accept the dollar. Then I ask if he can call me a cab. This is where I almost get into a fight with the bartender.

It's pushing one AM and I don't want to walk back to my car alone and unarmed. Those kids that yelled at me might still be hanging around. So my plan is to take a cab back to where I parked. When I try to explain this to the bartender, it takes him three repeats to understand I'm asking him to call me a cab, and then he says "Where to?"

"Oak and Bellevue."

"What?"

"I left my car at the corner of *Oak* and *Bellevue*."

"Look, if I'm going to call for a cab, I have to know where you're going, asshole."

"*Oak. And. Belle. Vue!*"

We're yelling in each other's faces, making no progress at all. It isn't until hours later that I realize he must have thought I was repeating vehemently "I don't want to tell you":

"Where's the cab going to?"
"*I won't tell you!*"

This is how it all starts, I'm thinking, the bar fights in all those trucker movies can be traced back to two people trying to understand each other over the jukebox. It's the only explanation I have for him getting so pissed off. He was ready to pull me across the bar until we were interrupted by two bouncers dragging a guy down the stairs, kicking him out because he threw up in the club — "Come back when you can hold your liquor!" The whole thing is ridiculous to me — you book a band named Tha Alkaholiks and you have to expect some vomit.

It takes six club employees to get this guy outside. "What did I do?" he's screaming, trying to blame it on the flu — "I'm sick! I'm *sick*!" Then his friends bust into the lobby and I'm at the periphery of a huge brawl that spills down the stairs and into the street. The bartender jumps in — he's forgotten his dispute with me and I call for a cab myself while he tackles the vomiter, who's escaped from the bouncers and is making a desperate run for the bar.

The concert is winding down and people on their way to the door jump in and start fighting without knowing who to hit or why. In the end, the vomiter is ejected and outside he and his friends throw beer bottles, hubcaps, whatever they find in the street at the windows of the club. "It's *plexiglass*, you dumb shits!" Cops are called, a bartender runs outside with a baseball bat, but it's too late. They're already gone — into the night, vigilantes off to defend the rights of people everywhere to puke in bars, restaurants, wherever they see fit.

Inside, the crowd explains the scene to each other. Even though it happened right there in front of us all, we want to describe the fight — "Man! Did you see what happened?" The owner is left trying to sort out the good guys from the bad, kicking out anybody who might have touched him during the scuffle — "You're out ... you're out ... nobody hits me in my club!"

"You hit me first!"

And then there it is — "Last Call." I hear the song like an echo, like I'm inside a tunnel, a coal mine, and it's being pumped in just for me. Nobody else downstairs even listens, but if they paid attention, they could hear it above the sirens — "It's time I roll my sleeves up, fuck a few MCs up, another rough cut from the crew that won't ease up." People are filling out police reports behind me and I stare at my reflection in that mirrored wall they seem to have behind so many bars, glimpses of part of my face in between Grand Marnier and Hennessey bottles — the true Alkaholiks experience. I see my chapped lips and drained expression from the heat of the crowd, from staking out my spot by the stage and standing strong as everyone converged around me, staying right in the middle of things for as long as I could.

Here downstairs it's a different effect. I flash forward to myself describing it to Danielle later, or writing it down, but I try to push all that out of my mind and just concentrate.

Twenty-four

Sitting on our front steps today, Danielle and I watch a Freezee Pops truck drive past and circle the apartment complex. I feel like saluting it. I feel some kind of pride in the company even though I only worked there for two days. I never even picked up my check.

It's been over a year since Danielle and I spent one February weekend cruising through run-down neighborhoods selling cones, which at the time felt like my greatest accomplishment. By walking into that ice cream office and writing down "college instructor" as prior work experience, I felt like I was stripping my new job of all its pretensions. Being an ice cream man, even for one weekend, canceled out the seriousness of my real job, and by not taking my real job too seriously, I was determined to stay who I was before. Which seemed like a good idea at the time.

Now, with most of our friends leaving, Danielle and I are thinking about the future. Danielle wants to go back to school. Temping has taken on its own kind of permanence, and she's ready to move on to something new, or back to something old, depending on how you look at it. Either way, I am not a fan of this idea. I asked her what kind of jobs she's been looking for, and she showed me a brochure for a master's program in higher education administration.

"Is that really what you want to go into?

"No, not really."

Danielle wants to open her own refuge for animals, or run a no-kill shelter, or volunteer at an animal refuge or no-kill shelter. But as much as I'm in support of not killing animals, this idea does not sit well with me. First, I haven't seen her do any research on animal refuges, so I don't know how seriously she's considering it. She has the grad school brochure, which tells me she's doing less job-hunting than hunting for ways to avoid a job. Second, I don't like the idea of being the only one of us with a paying job. "What would you do if you couldn't open an animal shelter? What would you do if you didn't go back to school?"

"I don't know, just get some job I hate, I guess. Like everybody else."

"I don't hate my job."

"Yeah. You're lucky."

"You could find a job like that too. You could teach."

"I don't want to teach. I just want to go to school or volunteer or something to take some time off."

"Then you need to stop buying stuff."

"I don't buy that much stuff." She's upset now, which upsets me.

"Maybe not, but you always want stuff. It's like all the time you have this consistent list of things you'd like to have. And you're always talking about them, asking if I think you could sell your blood for a few weeks and have enough to buy whatever it is."

"If I find ways to get extra money, I should be able to spend it on whatever I want."

"But that's just the thing, though. What you make you always consider extra money. What I make pays the bills and then you get to spend all yours on fun stuff."

"I get stuff for both of us with my money. I buy you things you want." It's true. She bought me an Alkaholiks CD this afternoon.

"You do, but it's like you always get to have fun with your money and mine just goes into the checking account."

"Why do you have to think of it as *your* money?"

We have had this argument before. It's the worst kind of fight, one about money. The kind of fight I overheard most nights as a kid and that would end sometimes with a chair smashed into a table, but more often with the slamming of doors. It's a fight about money, but also about so many things that go back to who we used to be when we met, me encouraging Danielle to do things and Danielle encouraging me to quit them.

Finally, I say, "If all you're doing is stalling, going back to school is a pretty expensive stall."

"We can live off what you make."

We can. We can live like we've lived so far. I make more now than both of us combined used to make. But now we have student loans to pay back, and now that I'm working I want to have some money, and not even so I can spend it. I just like the idea of having it in the bank. I get a salaried job and all the sudden I'm a kid with a shoebox full of twenties. I've found my place and now I'm incredibly impatient for her to find hers. She seems stunted to me, like she's spinning her wheels. I act like a baby about it.

We sit there not talking to each other and watch the Freezee Pops truck make its second, slower go-round, just like I learned in the Sales Techniques video. Then we see another familiar vehicle, our friend David's.

❈ ❈ ❈

We haven't seen David very often since the Halloween party he took us to. That night really did something to him. I haven't seen him wear the cowboy hat again and he's started going to church. He was making his way to the airport to pick up relatives coming in for his med school graduation ceremony, but he felt a pull toward our apartment and wanted to say hello, or more like goodbye. He's moving to Birmingham, Alabama, where he'll be a surgery resident, a real doctor. For a graduation present, we give him a boomerang.

David is already checking his watch, but he wants to hang out with us one last time before he moves, so he says he can spare an hour and a half. We take his new boomerang to Cherokee Park and immediately lose it in the creek. We can see it there, over the side, sort of half-floating just out of reach. My idea is to make our way around to the other side and then hook it with a tree branch or something, form a human ladder and rescue the boomerang. I get too excited, though. I run way ahead of David and Danielle on the path and I stretch too far and by the time they catch up I'm practically face-down in the mud, clutching onto a tiny tree and hoping it doesn't snap and send me into the water.

I'm rescued along with the boomerang, but within five minutes David has it stuck in a tree. We raid the back of his car and throw frisbees and bottles of Gatorade at the tree until it lets go of the boomerang and David almost hits a rollerblader as soon as he throws it — "Sorry man." He asks when we're going to start going to church, wants to know what shows we've been going to lately, now that he doesn't feel right hanging out in bars or clubs. He talks about how much he loves his new church and about how he's cleaned up his act and stopped drinking and cursing, when David was already one of the tamest, most upstanding people I knew. Like I said, people have described him as "all-American." It feels like I'm talking to someone else about David today, reminiscing about a friend of ours who used to dress up like a cowboy and pretend he knew how to repair our car stereo. It's like he decided all at once to change so much about himself, and something puts me off about that.

David wants to return everything he's borrowed and leave on good terms with his friends, so he's been making the rounds today. He brings us one rollerblade wrist guard and as many times as both Danielle and I assure him it's somebody else's, he wants to leave it here anyway. It's the effort that matters, I guess. He wants his bicycle helmet back, the one he'd said I could keep. Then he hugs us and leaves.

David and Chad are moving on, med school completed, diplomas in hand. It's official now. They are doctors. But they're still in training, working too-long hours for too-low wages and moving wherever they're told they have to. David will land in Birmingham and Chad not in New Orleans like he wanted, but in Toledo, at the Medical College of Ohio. Their departures will seem to stretch out forever with David driving back to Louisville to turn in a forgotten garage door opener, and me and Danielle visiting Chad on our trip to the Underground Publishing Conference, which will seem more subdued this year, but maybe I'm repeating myself. This summer has wrapped back around on the last one. I can see the pattern. One year later so many people have moved on, but I'm in the same place and it seems like the time in between could collapse, that it almost wouldn't exist if I hadn't documented it. But will this cycle continue? Or will it revolve into the distance like David's boomerang, not circling and coming back to us, but flying higher and further away, into treetops to be retrieved and then finally lost forever on somebody's roof in Birmingham.

Spring this year feels like an ending, but a welcome ending. I hadn't spoken to David in weeks. I was just waiting for him to stop by, secretly looking forward to the last time I would hang out with him. It's true. And I hate to even think about it that way, because the thing is, if you go looking for endings, you'll find them.

❊❊❊

The way things ended with Jake and Carrie was strange enough. I almost killed Jake on a state park swing set. He was trying to Superman like me, lying on the swings on our stomachs, arms outstretched. The problem was gravity. I weigh now probably what Jake weighed as a 6th grader, the biggest kid size these swings anticipated. Jake's body gave way at the apex of his swing, and hangs vertical in the air for one horrendous second, upside down, before crashing. His head hit first and seemed to support his full weight before his body toppled sickeningly to one side, forming what looked like an L. I helped him pick sand out of his eyelids. He told people at work that he walked into a tree.

This isn't the first time I've injured Jake. Not even the first time on a playground. There was renegade tennis, and midnight hiking, and backing over his foot with my car. If we were a couple, it would have looked like an abusive relationship. He lied to people to explain his sudden limp or to cover up getting whacked in the eye with a tennis racket. "I fell down the stairs." "I walked into a tree." People will only believe so much.

Jake and I were so young when we met. We didn't really know ourselves well enough to understand how to make someone else happy. Jake used to openly criticize Danielle's body, which she worried was too skinny, to make Carrie feel better about her own body, which she worried was too fat. Carrie began to respond to most things I said with "Well that's just your opinion." I would say, "I didn't like that movie," or "There are too many Applebees in this town," and she would respond, "That's just your opinion." I used to make fun of music she liked.

It was easy to hate each other, all of us married at 21 and confident in our respective relationships. We didn't need anybody else. We didn't even need to be particularly nice to each other, because at the end of the night I went home with Danielle and Jake went home with Carrie. Outside those pairs, we offered each other nothing but entertainment. All that connected us was a common appreciation for the band Pavement and a need to find something to do with our time outside the process of looking for someone to have sex with, which kept most people our age very busy.

The conflict that drives people's lives is the desire for relationships, and then the fucking up of those relationships. To end a romantic relationship is expected in the natural course of events. To end a friendship, though, makes you a bad person, intolerant of the flaws of others. As if friendships were truly forever, while marriages crumble around us. Friendship is interminable. That's why when couples split up they promise to still be friends.

Jake's swing set accident isn't the last time I see him, but it changes something between us. We stop calling each other very often, as when we do we're likely to turn down invitations. What happened to those people who would agree to go midnight hiking because Jake worked too late for the regular kind? Maybe it was my idea not to bring flashlights, and maybe I screamed "snake!" when it honestly could've been a shadow or a curvy stick. But does it really have to end like this? My best years of stolen street signs and playground violence, the bad ideas of our extended youth, all traded for a neck brace and some painkillers.

I think about driving to that Alkaholiks show alone, and the time I didn't go to an open mic reading on campus because none of them wanted to come with me. We are holding each other back. We make fun of Jake's work clothes, make fun of Kelly for going to bed at 10 PM so that she wouldn't be tired all day at work. They make fun of me for using the word "pedagogy" one night at a party. We don't want to see anyone change.

I think about Jake landing face-first in the sand, that first moment of horror when nobody moved, and those longer, more excruciating moments when Jake didn't move. What were we doing on that playground anyway? We were holding onto some idea of who we used to be, challenging each other to swing set stunts in our late twenties.

The problem was obvious. We were killing each other.

Twenty-five

Danielle and I spend the drive to visit Chad in Toledo talking about the master's program she's applying to. It feels good to see her getting more interested in something as unlikely as a degree in higher ed administration. There are classes about how universities are run and funded, where the money comes from and goes to, and the way the administration deals with scandals. All the behind-the-scenes, evil overlord stuff I know nothing about. For an idea that began as her way to avoid getting a job, I'm surprised by how interesting these classes sound, and I think she is too.

I try to put myself in her position, going back a few years to when I graduated and had no idea what I wanted to do. I did the same thing she's doing. College was all I knew, so I went back. I enrolled in an education program I had no interest in. I tried teaching high school and made myself miserable. I felt like there wasn't much out there for me. Since I started teaching college, though, I feel like this is where I'm supposed to be, and despite all my fears of getting stuck and burned out, it feels good to have found a job that I like. Danielle hasn't found that yet. The two central questions of most people's twenties are jobs and relationships. At least I've solved one of them. One of them came so easy. We were grown up so early and pretending not to be. But now I'm ready for it. And I'm ready to wait for her.

My friend Chad has known since middle school that he was going to be a doctor. I met him in seventh grade, and he was already talking about it then. And now he's doing his residency, cutting people open, saving lives, buying a house.

When Danielle and I get out of our rental car at Chad's new house, a girl across the street waves at us ceaselessly. She has a tire swing around her waist and she's leaning forward as far as she can, stretching both her arms out in a greeting. Chad rushes us inside. "That's the retarded girl across the street. Of course she takes an instant liking to me." He shudders, looks at her through the blinds. No matter how many medical courses Chad takes, he's squeamish as ever. He has a sincere phobia of the mentally challenged, and of midgets lately, he tells us, because of a dream he had where his dad was an evil midget.

It's Chad's birthday. Twenty-seven. He's a real doctor now, with a real salary. He has his own house, his own little piece of northern Ohio real estate. He has a carport. He has a fenced-in backyard complete with one shade tree and a giant mysterious hole. Danielle suspects it will keep growing and growing until it eventually swallows the house. Chad says he may buy a hammock. I say he should buy a goat. "Why else have a backyard?" I say. Danielle pictures the goat sleeping inside with him at night, curling up beside him on the couch. Chad pictures it eating his clothes.

On the inside, Chad's new house looks like a rearrangement of all his old stuff, plus housewarming gifts from his parents. He gives us the tour — the blue room, the red room — these colors are the reasons Chad bought this house. He sincerely told us there were other houses he liked better, but he went with the paint. "You two get to sleep in the red room tonight — it's kind of the guest room, and where I keep my laptop, and the laptop desk, which is the old desk I used to use with my computer. My *computer*, now, is kept in the blue room…" In the blue room he shows us his new, too-fancy glasstop desk and laser mouse, which he's discovered will not work together. "I think the laser reflects off the glass and won't register."

"Why don't you buy a mousepad, or a regular mouse?" Danielle asks.

"Then what's the purpose of having a glasstop desk?"

So it sits unused, on the floor beside his computer and his stereo, which is boxed up again, probably forever.

Chad's house is directly between the Medical College of Ohio and the University of Toledo campus. He likes UT better. We walk from his house to the campus. He wants to show us the architecture, the bike trail, the student center. We linger outside a building with an indoor pool. Chad leads us around the corner to stare at what he calls the frolic pool — "Not only do they have a pool for doing laps, they have a smaller frolic pool as well. Look at her in there, just frolicking. Probably just got her student ID." Chad has tried to get into this building before, but the door won't open without a valid UT student card. So he stands here, face and torso pressed against the giant window, fogging up the glass. "I wish I was just coming to college."

❈❈❈

Chad spends most of the day in orientations, where it is reinforced how many hours of his life will be spent at the hospital this year. "I have til next Thursday. That's pretty much it for me."

Tonight, though, Danielle and I take him to the kickoff party for this year's Underground Publishing Conference, twenty minutes south of Toledo in Bowling Green. Chad is amazed — "I haven't found anything to do here yet. You guys come from out of town and you have a whole evening lined up." When we show our IDs, Chad is offered a free drink because it's his birthday. The rest of the night, he scams free drinks. He scopes out different sides of the bar, waits for the first bartenders to go on break, waits for the shift to change. He drinks free all night. Danielle wins at pool.

I see some familiar faces from last year's conference, but it's a different crowd at the same time. Chad plays more pool with random people in the bar while Danielle and I go outside for a walk. "Maybe that fortune teller in New Orleans was wrong," I tell Danielle. "Chad seems pretty happy here." Visiting so soon after he moved doesn't feel like we're seeing each other *again* so much as just seeing each other. He seems a little different, though, even after just three weeks. Like he's been reborn. Toledo Chad. Or like a gangster name — Chaddy Toledo. I mean to tell him that one, because he'd like that one, but I forget to when we go back inside.

❈❈❈

In the morning I do my workshop session on zines in the college classroom. I am almost late for my own session because I'm so timid about parking in the faculty lot. Danielle drops me off with a box containing the final 100 copies of *El Cumpleanos de Paco*, plus zines my students made last semester. Donald's *Chickens Will Rule the World* — stories of Southern Indiana cops, of eating in a 24-hour diner that's really a trailer in somebody's back yard. Part of the assignment was to come up with a distribution plan, your own way of getting your work out there. Donald works as a package handler at UPS, so he drops copies at random into crates when he's on the job, sends them all over the world. His was one the best, the story and the distribution. I also love Kylee's zine that begins, "I never thought my job selling Mary Kay Cosmetics would lead to a night of wild sex..." I'm here to show off their work, and to talk about how folding and stapling together zines and finding ways to get them to people can a make student feel closer to their writing. It means more when it isn't just going into a file cabinet in the basement of the humanities building.

With Danielle parking the car, I make it inside on time. Soon, Danielle comes in, and five more people, and we start to talk. We talk, we debate, we share stories and secrets on this balmy morning in Bowling Green. As the fluorescent lights of the classroom buzz over our heads, we consider each other's viewpoints. Do zines belong in the college classroom, we ask. Does that kill their undergroundness, or does it introduce zines to people who might not have found them on their own? Could it bring new writers into the world of zines? Is it academics honing in on a subculture, or is it one way to keep that subculture going? We began to deepen our understanding, and to bite our lips and nod introspectively at that understanding. We drink free coffee provided by the Underground Publishing Conference. Someone sticks her head in the room and asks if there's decaf coffee and I say I don't know.

After the session, I set up my book table. I give away a few books. I trade freely with what anyone else has made or written. Danielle helps me create two stacks, labeled "Take Mine" and "Leave Yours." At the bottom of it all, we include "Or FREE," but some people still seem apprehensive.

When I was a kid, my favorite game was Store. I would set up our wooden picnic table with a display of useless goods and attempt to sell them to my sisters and our neighbors. Old toys I didn't want anymore, things I found in the yard. Years later I saw this game in adult form when Danielle and I rented a rural Kentucky cabin for our anniversary. A man sat in front of his rusted trailer, surrounded by scattered car parts, broken lawn chairs, and a sign that said STORE. I laughed at him then, but today I am doing the same thing.

This year the conference has taken a big interest in marketing and promotion, so much that they could have called it the Overground Marketing Conference. There are sessions on getting your publications reviewed by local newspapers, or getting your zines into libraries, which is great, but there are also sessions on high production values, which equals high cost, which equals charging your readers so you can recover that cost, which necessitates a marketing strategy.

I didn't invent zines, but I was stapling together my own writing for years before I even knew what a zine was. I thought I was the only one doing it, and I miss that. Maybe I shouldn't feel so possessive of the idea. Maybe I'm part of the problem, bringing zines into college writing classes. But I still don't like the turn this year's conference is taking. Some of it makes sense — it really does. But it all seems to perpetuate this idea that the underground isn't worth anything until the mainstream takes notice. That your book isn't legitimate until you make it look like it was produced by someone other than yourself. I can't understand it. Zines that would have cost one dollar last year, staple-bound, are now ten dollars and sickeningly glossy. They seem to be selling, though, faster than I can give away my free books at my unpopular table. The final 100, but I give away maybe twenty. Maybe.

Then, when I'm already feeling bad enough about being here, someone picks up *El Cumpleanos de Paco.* "You wrote this?"

"Yeah."

"Who's the publisher?"

"Me."

"Ok. Vanity press."

I hate this term vanity press. *Vanity* press. As if I'm so vain that no matter how bad my work is, or how many publishers turn me down, I will print it myself not out of determination or DIY spirit, but out of my own vanity. You don't hear the term used outside writing. There are no vanity films or vanity music. "Oh I don't listen to Fugazi. That's *vanity* punk rock." In those forms, independence is flourishing. The low-budget, the self-produced is the cutting edge. It's what breaks with tradition. Writing is dying because *it's* vain, because people want to write to some sense of intellectualism and cultural superiority that's tied up in the position literature held a century ago. The term vanity press is a slur, but all writing is vain. All art is self-involved, self-obsessed, and it disgusts me, but only in other people. Me, I sit at my table after the vanity press comment and I glare at all the *real* publishers, the tiny companies run by friends who publish each other, the incorporated indie press at the corner table.

Just one year ago I felt like I'd found my place here, but this isn't at all what I'm looking for. I get all worked up about it then I'm ok, then pissed off again.

❈ ❈ ❈

The next morning Danielle sleeps in while I go with Chad to get doughnuts. A Krispy Kreme worker leans across the counter and recites "Would you care for a complimentary fresh, hot, glazed Krispy Kreme?" A businessman jumps in front of us. "Can I have *three*?"

In the car we talk about Danielle's indecision, her feeling that there's no job out there that she wants. Chad talks about his upcoming residency. "This week is all orientation stuff. Then after that, well, I won't be spending much time at my house." He gets paid a little over forty thousand. Not bad for a residency, he says, but it breaks down to something like nine dollars an hour.

"So what made you want to go into all this?"

"Um, my mom. To some extent. And also back in high school and junior high, mostly high school when I really, really enjoyed school, I thought I wanted to do something that would let me stay in school for a long time. Now I'm kind of rethinking that." He looks like he means it. "What about you?"

The Only Monkeyfucker on the Web

I was teaching in a run-down computer lab in the basement, across the hall from the part-time lecturers' office. I started teaching during this brand new initiative to incorporate technology with writing instruction. I got really excited about the whole thing. I set up a class homepage with a messageboard where I could post assignments or announcements and students could communicate with me and respond to each other's writing.

Soon we realized that anyone fucking around on the Internet could access our board, and we started getting posts from all over. Somebody tried to hook us all into a pyramid scheme selling used tires, I got a mean letter from someone in Great Britain, and an anonymous poster called Jared a "stupid stupid monkey fucker." Still today if you go to most search engines and type in "stupid stupid monkey fucker," our English 101 messageboard is the only site that comes up.

Jared suspected his enemies from high school. His classmates stuck up for him, made fun of the intruder's spelling, and the whole thing escalated to the point where I got dragged into it. The way the board was set up, you could type anything you wanted into the username box, so we started to see posts like "Class is cancelled. I got the shits — Mickey," followed by "Still incapacitated. Won't be back. Everyone's getting an A." Seems like a harmless joke, but you'd be surprised how many people took it seriously. Students would call me in office hours to find out if we legitimately didn't have class anymore. We still had over a month left in the semester, but I guess these imagined shits were so severe they had put me out of commission for good.

Remember to wash your hands, kids. There's a case of the permanent shits going around.

How I Got into Teaching in the First Place

"Student teacher" doesn't make sense grammatically. It's redundant, like "School of Education," which is where I found myself a few weeks after receiving an undergraduate degree in English. I needed a job. Four years of student loan bohemia had left me twenty thousand dollars in debt, and with nothing in the way of work experience. I wanted to write, but not *for* anyone. Other than that, all my prospects felt like moving backward, from living for free to spending my time doing something I hated for money.

So I felt like I was joining the Army instead of applying to graduate school. I was there because I was desperate, and they were ready to feed off that desperation. A lot of things about student teaching reminded me of the Army, or at least my perception of it based on movies and old Gomer Pyle episodes. I had to get up unbelievably early, maintain a crisp, clean appearance, and follow pretty much any order they gave me. I finished my orientation courses and was sent into the public school system pathetically undertrained. We spent a few weeks observing the real teachers who offered to let us sit in their classrooms, and we were required to submit a detailed report each day. Before long, I started to realize that these reports were used only to prove I was there and I was paying attention, which is pretty much what was required of the high school students.

I first taught during summer school. I woke up at 7 AM to spend hours reading Merchant of Venice out loud with these students only a few years younger than me, these poor fucking people sentenced to spend July and August trapped inside the same building they spent too many days avoiding during the regular school year. That's why most of them were there — too many absences. I understood. I wanted to skip every day too. I felt uneasy, like I was part of the system that was killing their summer. And when the bell rang at the end of the day, I beat most of them out to the parking lot.

I was an awful student teacher. I had no idea what I was doing at all, and had no desire at all to use what little authority my title may have given me. So I kept my mouth shut when students raided a supply closet during our field trip to the *Courier-Journal*, blocked the view of their regular teacher while they stuffed their pockets with glue sticks and post-it notes. Jesus, I felt sorry for the kids. It was like they were in prison instead of school. At least let them have some souvenirs to take home. But still I tried to develop some hint of a professional demeanor. I didn't laugh when students made fun of me or each other, no matter how fucking clever it was. I tried to smooth things over with the school librarians after Elizabeth called them a couple of butt buddies. I even learned to feign absolute excitement for *Merchant of Venice*.

Not having much practice lecturing, I usually covered in one day what the regular teacher had intended to stretch into a week-long unit. I felt so uneasy in front of the classroom that any period of silence, no matter how brief it was, would make me question if I was doing something wrong. So I sped through the material, and when no one jumped at responding to one of the real teacher's pre-written questions, I'd answer it myself, or move on without answering if it were a really hard one and I was afraid I might get it wrong.

On top of our classroom duties, student teachers were encouraged to play a meaningful role in the school community. Our first project was called "Hands Across Manual High School." In our assigned classrooms, we passed out construction paper and gave each student time to trace an outline of his or her hand, write a name on it, and cut it out with a pair of dull scissors. The student teachers then collected these construction paper hands. We spent an entire afternoon taping them side-to-side throughout the halls, almost too high but not quite for the basketball players to write "homo" and "ass pounder" underneath each other's names. The project was supposed to somehow celebrate diversity, although I was never quite sure how. Diversity of hand size, maybe.

Two Reasons I Can No Longer Teach High School:

#1. William S. Burroughs Incident — Cut-up Poems Created by an 11th Grade English Class Using Several Editions of the Student Newspaper and One Copy of a Gay Cruising Publication that Someone Sneaked Into the Stack

Interviews with the principals

Mr. Osborne's reflections on this school year were interesting: "My penis is around six inches. The ninth graders will catch on soon. Large penises are neither rare nor special." What he likes best about the school is going down, because some gay men can't get past penis worship.

This year there have been many changes in our school. Guys meet guys, principals and students shower together. Mr. Warren feels this is a great program to improve attendance. "We like to and will treat kids like adults." Mr. Warren was also asked about his role as vice-principal. He says that he would like to help school clubs have more field trips, dry kissing, massage, and mutual masturbation — "I have seen a penis as big as sixteen inches!" Mr. Warren's hobbies include racecar driving, fishing, and oral sex on a man without a condom.

Are You into Hardcore S&M?

4-H is seeking several gay males to do their thing. More specifically, its objectives are anal intercourse without condom and spermicide, using drugs, and selling candy. The money will be used to pay for analingus.

Potential 4-H members must have certain qualifications: no fats, please. Fems OK, petite even better. Hairy body a plus. Just a bunch of real men, saying every hot, sexy thing that's on their minds.

#2 Mocking the Holocaust

April 1st — one week until my term as student teacher is over, and there isn't much left in the regular teacher's book of lesson plans. I've already rushed through *A Doll's House* and *Heart of Darkness*, and none of my own ideas for the curriculum are very well received after the Burroughs incident. It's starting to get warm again outside and I spend as much time looking longingly out the window as any of the students do. I wish we could just go home.

This morning my mentor teacher comes in with a new assignment — students will design butterfly patterns and cut them out of construction paper. She has me read them some kind of nationwide mission statement: "To commemorate a dark period in world history, a group of teachers seeks to collect one butterfly for each child who died in the Holocaust." An elementary school in New York initiated the project, and we're going to mail them our butterflies so the younger kids could dump ("release") them off the roof of their school.

Out of guilt, if nothing else, my entire class starts working solemnly on their butterflies, trying to get the symmetry just right, waiting patiently for the non-dried-up markers so they can decorate the wings. An hour passes and nearly everyone has created five or six butterflies to contribute to the Holocaust memorial. The glue and scissors are back in the cabinet and everyone feels like their time here today wasn't wasted, like they've been part of something. "Great work," I say. "I have just one more announcement before we go..." As I had watched everyone work so intently, I saw the opportunity for a joke that I just couldn't let pass — "*April Fool's!*"

The students stop cramming books into their backpacks and look up at me blankly. "Come on," I continue, "do you really think we could cut out enough butterflies to match all the kids who died in the Holocaust? That'd be like a million butterflies!"

My plan is to give them just a second to feel ripped off, and then to reassure them that the project is completely legitimate. But things get confusing when the regular teacher jumps in to reprimand me. "He's not serious! Mr. Hess, tell them it was a joke!"

So I say in sort of a forced manner, "Yeah, it was all a joke," then the bell rings before I can explain any further. Some students seem to understand what I mean is that the *joke* was a joke, but more of them leave the room believing the entire butterfly/holocaust thing that was my harsh April Fool's Day prank. There is some glaring and muttering as they file out of the classroom. One kid stomps past me and huffs "I can't believe we cut out all those fucking butterflies for nothing."

But here I am again talking about my fuckups, things that were funny about teaching high school, and truthfully these are very isolated instances, the few entertaining stories from all those miserable months. I used to go for long latenight walks around my dangerous apartment complex with Danielle, her listening to me complain about work and understanding that I wanted her to listen, not offer solutions or suggestions for dealing with all of it, not give bullshit advice like I always give her. We'd walk for hours, in circles around Mt. Vernon Apartments and the red brick buildings that all look the same. Every night for six months was the same — we were out when it was freezing, bundled up in scarves and toboggans, me praying for a fucking snow day and then back up at 7 to work the next morning.

And when those six months ended, I walked away happier to leave the place than when I got out of high school for the first time. I stumbled across the street and the English department said, "Hey, you wanna teach college?" That's how I got into it. I've never made any strong decisions that have brought me to where I am now. Honestly I feel like my best decisions are when I choose *not* to do something. I've always felt like things carry me along and when I want to say fuck it, I can. I can avoid things, but not change them or create them. Does that make any sense? I got into this job accidentally, luckily, as much as David went to med school because his dad went to med school, or as much as Chad went to med school because he likes money. But I remember back further than that, to when I lived with Shane and took classes like Fitness Walking and The History of Country Music, when I never went to class, but knew sincerely and for whatever reason that I wanted to be a college professor.

Twenty-six

From: GuinnessBinge@gmail.com
To: Hess, Mickey S
Sent: Tue 4/12/2002 9:31 PM
Subject: Academic Journals

Mickey

    How would I get published in a journal? I want to come up with a great paper on writing and theories thereof. If I do, I'd want it to be published just so I'd start gaining credibility now so I could be better prepared for a writing job or something when I graduate. Besides, I want to do something great. Live up to my potential I guess. If you'd like to collaborate that would be cool. lol you could give all the ideas and I could agree, that would be genius! Really though Im serious, I need some help and it sounds fun. Correct me if Im wrong though.

Dylan

    I was surprised to get this email from Dylan Barrett, a student in my Introduction to College Composition course. He wouldn't even read anything from an academic journal in class, much less try to get published in one.

    When I first met Dylan he was standing outside my classroom, trying to over-enroll in English 101 three weeks after the deadline. The university's writing placement exam had stuck Dylan in remedial composition, not because he lacked any skill, but because he refused to take the exam seriously. They asked him to write an essay describing a challenge he'd faced and overcome in his life, and he set it up as a dialogue between fast-food chain mascots. It sounded like something I would have done.

Three weeks into the lowest level remedial writing course, Dylan was tired of discussing the role of the comma, and his instructor was sick of Dylan's fifteen-page mock-political tracts against the practice of diagramming sentences. "Speakers of English, liberate yourselves today." So instead of failing him for not satisfying the assignments and sentencing him to repeat remedial composition, Dylan's instructor took his case to the English department, and the English Department sent him to me. Dylan didn't take my assignments seriously either — he refused to write anything that required research and he refused to even step into the library — but he handed me a 200-page novel he'd written, and he sent me an email asking how he could get published in one of those journals he wouldn't read.

Everything about how Dylan approached things was so wrong, but he was so sure of himself and genuinely excited about everything he wrote. But they don't give points for excitement on the placement exam. In an era of standardized testing and No Child Left Behind, there's no room left for a student like Dylan. An eighteen-year-old novelist gets left behind.

This is a problem.

It makes me want to start a student reading series where Dylan can write and read whatever he wants. It makes me want to collaborate with him to co-author an article about writing from the student's and teacher's perspectives. He hands me ten pages by the end of the first week. It's good stuff. He's making me think about what my job means, and he's reminding me how it felt when I was on the other side of the educational equation.

We're really doing it. We're going to send it to *Composition Studies*. It's going to be something.

But soon enough I stop hearing from Dylan. He drops out of IU Southwest to become manager at a check-cashing place down the street.

❋ ❋

This has been a weird semester. Dylan's disappearance and a conversation with another student have shaken the foundations of what I am doing with my life. The conversation happened in my American Lit class, while students were working in groups, trying to determine what Flannery O'Connor meant by the *moment of grace*. I was sitting in the back of the room, listening in on their group discussions, when a very quiet student named Pranav approached me.

"Can I ask you a question?"

"Sure."

He opened his book to the story we'd read for class. "Why would somebody write this?"

"Good question," I said. "You always want to consider a writer's purpose."

But I'd misunderstood him. He shook his head. "No. I mean, why would someone even *write* like a story or an essay?"

And with that question, it all flashed before me: all that graduate school, all my years of reading and writing going back to my mom smiling at me as I sounded out Dr. Seuss — he might as well have asked me why people breathe or blink or fall in love. I was too caught up in it. I know literary criticism and narrative theory. I know the cognitive stuff from my education classes. And I could have quoted that stuff, but I could not come up with a decent answer for Pranav.

✿ ✿

Pranav's question and the few pages that Dylan and I wrote together before he left school for the work force got me thinking about what my role is here. Should I make the application of the things I teach more explicit, or is half of the learning process finding your own ways to apply the things you learn to your life, no matter how many years that takes you? Or does it just feel that way to me because my job entails teaching new people the things I learned? Does everyone else forget what they learn? Do they find that they never needed to know any of it in the first place?

The antithesis of Dylan's story is Mike Smith. Mike was a student in one of the first writing classes I taught, and now, four years later, he's teaching part-time at a college in South Louisville. The academic cycle of life is complete.

Dylan made me think about starting a student reading series, but it was Mike who helped make it happen. Mike talked to his students, I talked to mine, and it turned out that plenty of students had written things that they wanted to stand up in front of people and read. Mike and I talked to a local coffee-shop owner and created the Bean Street Reading Series, held every other Thursday night in New Albany, Indiana. Students read stories and poetry. We had Choose Your Own Adventure Night. We had a costume party. Local newspapers came out and took pictures.

The most amazing thing that can happen to a writing teacher is to be genuinely jealous of something your student wrote. It happens at Bean Street Café while I sit in the audience watching the end-of-the-semester reading. It happens with Mike's story about a grown man getting a toy soldier stuck in his nose, and with Dave's tale of being forced to apologize for making a girl throw up when he was in third grade.

I had been impressed enough with their work in the classroom, but to see it spoken, *performed*, to see the small crowd react to it — it was like I hadn't been paying attention before, like I just hadn't heard it the right way. The night-school students are all dead-on, from Bill who dresses up in a farm boy outfit and reads as his character Wally P. Hoglash, to Paul the Methodist preacher who writes stories that border on pornography. The series develops a small following. We have regular audience members who bring friends back with them and ask to hear Paul read last week's story again. Maybe this is why we write things, Pranav — to see if somebody is listening.

❋ ❋ ❋

From: Sebring, Marcia K
To: Hess, Mickey S
Sent: Tue 4/22/2002 2:48 PM
Subject: Congratulations
Congratulations! The Research & Grants Committee has named you a recipient of an Indiana University Southwest Teaching Award. Thank you for your commitment to our students' learning.

Sincerely,
Marcia Sebring,
Vice Chancellor for Academic Affairs

I've always had the fear that no matter what kind of success I achieve through my job, it will always be replacement success, and it will feel bad in a way because it's stealing something away from writing books and what I've always wanted to be good at. All my time that goes into teaching feels like time that I could have spent writing. I feel guilty when I stay up late reading student stories instead of writing my own. So normally when I receive some kind of recognition for the work I've done there's some anxiety along with it, but with this teaching award there's none of that. I read the notification letter ten times yesterday — The Indiana University Southwest Award for Excellence in Writing

Instruction. I know it's an empty word, but it sounds nice, better than *competence*, or *sufficiency*.
Excellence.

On campus, a man in overalls is jabbing at a raccoon with a broom handle. The raccoon is trapped inside the foyer of the IU Southwest library building, and as the broom handle comes toward him, he is hanging from a door frame by one front paw, using the other to swipe viciously not at the handle, but at the face of the man wielding it. The man is laughing at the raccoon's defense, then looks suddenly terrified.

I was finally given an office. My own office — the coveted holy grail for lecturers. I put up my Salvador Dali poster. Danielle helps me paint the walls Nautilus Blue, which comes out looking more like gothic black.

My office isn't in the choicest location, not in the humanities building or even anywhere near another instructor's office. I'm in the library. They gutted the study carrels and built me a little room in the dark back corner of the library stacks. The office itself isn't bad. It's huge, actually, bigger than offices in other buildings. It has 1960s carpet, still a blinding avocado green after decades of being covered by carrels and library shelves. The walls don't go all the way up because they didn't want to install a separate heating vent. When I talk to students in office hours, a library patron invariably walks up and closes my door, or asks us to talk more quietly.

In this office, time is linear, and it adds up. All those semesters that I spent as an academic hobo, carrying everything I owned on my back, it felt like a job benefit that I wasn't stuck at one desk all day, and that I could go home and have lunch with Danielle and then finish my work late at night after she went to sleep. There was some freedom in transition. But now that I have an office, I realize how much time I actually spend working. I'm here forty hours, sometimes longer, and I'm not getting as much done. Nowhere near as much. Who knows how many hours I was working back then?

The library closes at five on Fridays and I don't have my own key. The door locks behind me when I go downstairs to buy peanut M&Ms, and to get back in I have to go to campus police and convince them to let me into my office. Last week they said no. This week I have an IU Southwest faculty ID card. I'm official now. I had avoided the card for as long as I could, but here it is, a laminated image of my head floating in front of the IU Southwest clock tower, one of five backgrounds I could choose from. I look shifty in the picture. "Look straight ahead," the photographer told me. Then at the last minute, "No, over here."

As good as it feels to get the teaching award, I still feel restless on campus, like I just don't belong here. To the other members of the English Department, I'm the new guy who painted his office black, the young upstart who ties strings to trees and walks around campus with a box full of lizards. They've never watched me teach, but they have a distinct feeling I'm doing it wrong. They acknowledge the award, but I think it makes them suspicious. They offer some muttered congratulations at a department meeting, then everyone's quiet until one of the professors says, "Well we're all great at teaching."

No matter how many fliers I hang up or how many of their students invite them, the other members of the English department don't come to the Bean Street Reading Series, aside from a few exceptions. The retiring Henry James expert is a regular audience member. "I'm glad the department is sponsoring this," he told me.

They aren't.

The Medievalist, in fact, told me that, "It's good to let the students have their fun, but make sure they understand how it's different from serious literature."

The poet dropped by my office to tell me that spoken word is what's ruining poetry. "You can fool your audience with the performance," he said, "but on the page the poem might be terrible."

What?

This year I break down and attend the English Department Retreat, letting go of that last shred of resistance I was clinging to. We all drive an hour and a half to Pleasant Hill, Kentucky's Shaker Village, "America's largest restored Shaker community, where a remarkable society once flourished." It isn't all that remarkable. They hire local high school kids to dress up in straw hats and pretend to churn butter. We used to come here on field trips when I was in second grade.

I still can't understand the concept of a retreat. "So we're leaving our usual workplace to lock ourselves in a hotel room for two days and talk about work?" But nobody listens. They're excited about weekend brainstorming sessions. They're excited to combine work with their leisure time, when I want to keep the two as separate as possible.

This question of how I spend my time is at the heart of everything I have done this year. I don't want to feel like I'm sitting through my life, waiting for the end of the workday so I can go home and see Danielle and our animals, waiting for the end of the week so I can go home and write. I thought I had found a job that made me responsible for creating something or making things happen instead of just sitting in one place for eight hours a day. I thought I had found a job that let me manage my own time instead of punching in and out when I go on break. But somehow I let that system trap me. I work unaccounted-for hours at home, and now here I am spending a weekend discussing standardized testing at Shaker Village.

I drink the free Shaker coffee till my kidneys hurt and my temples throb, but it beats being lulled into self-hatred by brainstorming ideas for what to name the English department newsletter. At dinner, I eat as much shoo-fly pie as possible, and I sneak out of the restaurant, check out of the hotel, and drive home.

Back home, in bed with Danielle and our cats, I dream that I go up to the roof of the Humanities Building and throw my computer over the side. I do it out of frustration. I do it to get back at something. I do it for the same reason I started driving the ice cream truck. In the dream, the rest of the department is just getting back from the retreat, so they're all standing at the edge of the parking lot when the computer smashes into the sidewalk.

No one says anything. They just stare back up at me and I know I am going to be fired.

I wake up with this sick, terrified feeling that makes me drive immediately back to Shaker Village in time for the second day of the retreat. No one even knew I had left, and I sneak out again around lunch time. The feeling, though, sticks with me for a few days. Is keeping this job really that important to me? The anxiety I used to feel about taking this job has now given way to anxiety I feel about losing it, even though I'm not entirely happy here. When I accepted this full-time teaching job, I had this fear that my life so far had been me becoming who I am, and from here on out things will be pretty much the same. I thought I could resolve it by driving an ice cream truck or working the ball pit at Action World, and in some ways it worked. One job, one weekend at a time to break the routine.

When I took this job I was afraid it would take over my life, but now it has become part of my life. Teaching is becoming as much a part of what I do as writing. It's getting harder to separate the two, which makes it harder to ignore all the problems that come with it. I love what I do, but I'm less certain that IU Southwest is the place to do it. As much as I'll miss these students, I can't see myself staying here forever.

I'm a 27-year-old man. I have a wife, two cats, and an iguana. I spend my time reading student papers or writing my own papers about rappers who wear masks. Hip hop theory. Rap criticism. Am I the same person I was twelve years ago in my bedroom explaining Humpty Hump mythology to my little sister, or would I totally not impress myself? Does it make sense to feel proud of what I do for a living? In my office, black walls contrast with the mountain of paper my students and I have produced this year. Outside my office, in the library, the doctoral dissertations get thicker and thicker as the dates get closer to now. The more writing you do, the more there is to build from. One of the older professors broke his leg last week carrying a stack of books so high that he couldn't see over them. Is anybody even reading this stuff other than to fulfill class assignments or write new dissertations out of it? Where does it all end?

Thanks

To all the students I've been lucky to work with in Kentucky, Indiana, and New Jersey. You've taught me a lot about writing: Mike Smith, Jason Jordan, Adam Barrett, Chad Blevins, Christeen Amburgey, Jay Whitman, Clint Waskom, Andrew Walker, Beth Thomas, Simon McKim, Kyle Herman and Jana Morgan, Laura Ellis, Paul Hankins, Andrew Kaspereen, Karly Hamburg, Alexa Orduz, Liz Ryan, Robin Barletta, Carl Griesser, Matt Cohen, Janine Vasconcelos, Corey Meyers, Alex Sharry, Rance Robeson II, Glen Binger, Laura Sickle, Shavon Keller, Lisa Engel, Lisa Flynn, and so many others. If I forgot your name here, it is only because I learn one hundred new names every semester, and I have only so much space in my brain.

Thanks also to: Danielle Hess, Joe Meno, Al Burian, Todd Dills, Sean Carswell, G.K. Darby, Sarah Reidy, Lauren Cerand, Quimby's Bookstore in Chicago, Mac's Backs in Cleveland, Boxcar Books in Bloomington, IN, Jerry Gibson, The Rider University English Department, Andy Sturdevant, Katie Beach, Chris Dickens, Luke and Kelly Buckman, Kirsten and Will Armstrong, Adam White, Tracy Heightchew, Chad Patterson, Charlie Rose, Ron Whitehead, Michael Dean Odin Pollock, Bragi Olafsson, and Mike Smith again.

About the Author

Mickey Hess taught part-time for several universities in Kentucky and Indiana before moving to his current position as Assistant Professor of English at Rider University. His books include *Icons of Hip Hop: An Encyclopedia of the Music, Movement, and Culture* (Greenwood, 2007), and *Is Hip Hop Dead? The Past, Present, and Future of America's Most Wanted Music* (Praeger, 2007). His writing has appeared in *Ninth Letter, Punk Planet,* and *Created in Darkness by Troubled Americans: Best of McSweeney's Humor Category*. He lives in Philadelphia.

Marquis Book Printing Inc.

Québec, Canada
2008